Rosicrucian Manual

PRINTED IN THE UNITED STATES OF AMERICA
BY THE FLAME PRESS, INC.

"Because strait is the gate
and narrow is the way which
leadeth unto life, and few
there be that find it .☙☙.

Rosicrucian Manual

For the Instruction of Postulants in the
Congregation of the Outer, Neophytes, and
Fraters of Duly Instituted Colleges of the

Societas Rosicruciana In America

Written and compiled by

Khei, △X

Authorized by the High Council,

S∴R∴I∴A∴

Done into print and published
for the S∴R∴I∴A∴, by the
Flame Press, at the Sign of the
Rose Bush, on Manhattan
Isle., in the City of New York.
M   C   M   X   X.

Nihil Obstat;

Nestorius, X°,   Praemonstrator.
Paracelsus, IX°, Cancellarius.

Attest;

Reficio, IX°, Secretary General.

May, 1920.

New York City.

Preface

✠

In compiling this Manual for the use of members of the Societas Rosicruciana In America, there has been no intent of offering an occult treatise of any sort whatsoever. It is purely a manual of instruction and information for the exclusive use of members. It is not secret, but it is expected that each member will exercise due caution in exposing this or any other publication of the Fraternity in ways that may result in causing misunderstanding and give undesirable publicity to the principles of our Art.

In this manual will be found, first of all an amplification of Official Publication No. 2, entitled, "Who may become members of the S∴R∴ I∴A∴" This amplification is for the information of members themselves, and their guidance and instruction in seeking "heirs" or prospective members of the Fraternity.

The Ancient Landmarks are given in full, together with the Constitution of the Societas Rosicruciana In America, with which every member is required to be thoroughly familiar, for it is in consonance with these instruments that all legislative and executive work of the Fraternity in the United States is carried on.

Valuable matter is reprinted from "In the Pronaos of the Temple" by Dr. Franz Hartman, and also from "The Real History of the Rosicrucians" by Mr. Arthur Edward Waite. Both these valuable works are long since out of print, otherwise we should refer our members to the originals. It is essential however, that each member be familiar with these statements of the fundamental principles and legenda of the Fraternity at the very beginning of the study of our Art.

Some features may appear to be unnecessary repetition, but such instances will be found to be really advisable in order to give an accurate facsimile reprint or an obvious reason for the immediate context.

Initiates will readily understand the statement regarding the lack of evidence of a "visible organization," in the chapter entitled "Rosicrucian Orders." This chapter, valuable in many ways, sufficiently so to entitle it to publication in our manual, nevertheless shows unmistakable signs of Dr.

Hartmann's theosophical bias, especially in his reference to Paracelsus and the lack of indication that any organized society of true Adepts calling themselves "Rosicrucians" existed in his time. This bias is further borne out by his future references to India, the usual ultima thule of Theosophy. Rosicrucianism, we may say in passing, is distinctly the Egyptian Wisdom Teaching, and many critics and bibliographers with decided pro-Indian inclinations have failed to grasp this essential point. Neophytes after being advanced to the Zelator Degree are no longer confused by the concept that the Brotherhood has no visible organization. Decidedly, it has not.

It should be further noted that both Dr. Hartmann and Mr. Waite treat of the Rosicrucians, from knowledge apparently gleaned from the "Rosicrucian Classics" as we shall call the famous writings which are reprinted in this manual. It is the teaching of the Brothers, however, that Rosicrucianism is a synthesis of Religion, Science and Philosophy, and is really the renaissance of an ancient world-religion far antedating even that of the Egyptians, yet in making this statement it must be distinctly understood that the exoteric Fraternity has not, and does not claim to have any documentary evidence of continuous existence from such remote times. Many such fanciful claims have been made by impostors, but no convincing proof can be adduced. The Fraternity, even in the exoteric, has an undoubtedly great antiquity of origin and the principles of our Art have assuredly been maintained continuously from Atlantean times, but this form of continuity is vastly different from the impossible, illogical claims of documentary, organic continuity through human instrumentality.

It is earnestly hoped that every member of the Fraternity will make a careful study of this manual and become thoroughly conversant with the Constitution, Principles and Classics, for frequent allusion thereto will be made in the authorized Instructions and Degrees of the Order.

Contents

✠

𝔗∴𝔗∴𝔊∴𝔒∴𝔗∴𝔖∴𝔐∴𝔒∴𝔗∴𝔘∴

✠   ✠   ✠

Who May Become Members

of the

S∴R∴I∴A∴

This question is so frequently asked that it is expedient to put its comprehensive answer into print, for the personal guidance of members; for those who are occupied with prospective applicants, and for the information of all others into whose hands it shall legitimately come.

Any man from the age of twenty-one, and any woman from the age of sixteen is eligible to membership when the Congregation of Examiners is fully satisfied as to the applicant's moral character, mental fitness, intellectual caliber, and spiritual desires.

EXCEPTIONS.

The Fraternity does not permit, seek or knowingly encourage applications for membership by professional mediums, business psychics, soothsayers, fortune-tellers and fraudulent astrologers.

The Fraternity places a high valuation upon properly developed psychical and spiritual powers, and honest astrological science and skill. All other requirements being satisfied, the Fraternity gladly welcomes honest psychics and astrologers in private life to its membership; enjoining them, however, most emphatically against the use or mention of the Fraternity's name or their personal membership as a possible means of securing patronage, or claiming any endorsement by the Order.

The Fraternity reserves the right and privilege of endorsing within the confines of its own membership, the psychical powers or astrological skill of such of its members as it deems fit to be regarded as helpers of humanity, but it does not permit the use of its membership privileges for advertising purposes under any condition whatsoever.

Fraters and Sorores are especially cautioned against encouraging, seeking or advising the application for membership by any one, who, after careful consideration, they do not feel assured will become spiritually, psychically, intellectually, and temperamentally an harmonious member of the Society's fabric.

Members are especially cautioned not to seek the application of irresponsible persons. Without singling out any cult in particular, it has been noted that those who are most ardent in professing so-called "liberal thought" and extreme radical views manifest a tendency to disregard obligations solemnly assumed when subsequent events render it desirable for them to discontinue their affiliation with a given society. The S∴R∴I∴A∴ does not desire this class of members. It is open to those who approach the matter seriously, and will assume the necessary obligations honestly and sincerely, and who will show due respect for the same when once assumed.

Never urge a person to apply for membership solely on account of personal friendship; never seek to convert a person to the principles of the Order merely to secure his possible affiliation with us.

Only those who by training, education, and mental and spiritual aspirations are receptive to the FIVE AFFIRMATIONS, are qualified to become desirable members of the Fraternity.

Let it be understood above all else, that the Fraternity does not accept members for the purpose of developing mediums. Independent development and unfoldment forms an important part of our Work and Art, but no person can "join and start developing." Only after mastering the "Rosicrucian Fundamentals," passing the Zelator Degree as an Initiate Member of the First Grade, and showing proficiency in the Hermetic Teachings, is a member eligible to enrolment in the Alchemical Section for personal unfoldment and no exceptions will be made to this rule except by H.·.C.·.Dispensation.

NOT A FORUM FOR DEBATE.

Let it be positively understood by each applicant and each member that Collegiate Convocations are not open forums for general discussion, airing of personal views or exploitation of personal theories on political, sociological or economic subjects, however deep and sincere the convictions underlying such theories may be.

All argument, controversy, and debate are strictly forbidden and tabooed in the Adytum.

No single practice, rule, custom, ritual, or landmark can be changed or abrogated to suit the whims or personal feelings of any individual member.

The Landmarks of the Order forbid the Fraternity to question a frater or soror regarding personal religious beliefs, nor does it take any cognizance of such whatever.

In view of the above, and that there may be no misunderstanding, let it be known that this Fraternity is not in affiliation or sympathy with any sort of antagonistic religious propaganda. It is neither anti-Catholic, anti-Protestant, or anti-Semitic. It regards all such propaganda as effective barriers to the unity that should be obvious among truly religious people and such religious antagonism will in the larger percentage of cases be found to be the result of ignorance regarding the religion opposed, personal prejudice, fanaticism or bigotry. Such characteristics are not desirable attributes of those who seek to follow the teachings by the Master of the New Dispensation which were in complete accord with those of the prophet Malachi of the Old Dispensation in the memorable lines, "Have we not all one Father? Hath not one God created us? Why do we deal treacherously every man against his brother? (Mal. ii, 10.) The Rosicrucian Brotherhood has no place for religious fanaticism or religious fanatics. The Brotherhood distinctly utilizes and teaches the Principle and the Practice of the GOOD (GOD) that is in all religions.

In view of the number of applicants for admission to this Fraternity who already hold or have held membership in other organizations, we want to make as clear and unmistakable as possible the following condition of acceptance in the S.·.R.·.I.·.A.·. Membership in this Fraternity is contingent upon a whole-hearted, sincere desire to obtain the Rosicrucian Teaching and a mental attitude unbiased and unprejudiced by any previous or existent system of instruction elsewhere. The Societas Rosicruciana In America does not accept or regard as criteria any of the systems promulgated by any occult school, "Great School," present Theosophical cults or Spiritualism. THIS STATEMENT IS NOT MADE IN ANY SPIRIT OF ANTAGONISM OR CRITICISM, but simply because many students are inhibited in their advancement by a spirit of comparison of apparently closely correlated systems of teaching, accepting some points, rejecting others, until it is hopeless for them to expect to make adequate progress. One cannot reach a distant city travelling two distinct and separate routes at the same time. One MUST reject the one and follow the other.

Those who enter the Fraternity and then accept the Teachings only in so far as they accord with those of some previous teacher or school had better remain with the system or teacher of their first choice. Critical comparison does not make for progress and does make for inharmony.

IT IS ASSUMED AND MUST BE UNDERSTOOD that ALL who enter the Rosicrucian Brotherhood do so FOR ONE PURPOSE ONLY—to study and receive the Rosicrucian Philosophy. Advancement to the higher degrees is contingent upon the individual member's acceptance of the truths inculcated and willingness to take active part in the furtherance of the Great Work.·

REGULAR ATTENDANCE REQUIRED.

Members are also reminded that mere payment of dues in the Fraternity DOES NOT CONSTITUTE MEMBERSHIP IN GOOD STANDING. Only those who by reasonably regular attendance upon the Stated Convocations manifest an active interest and intimate participation in the work will be regarded as placing a valuation upon their privilege of membership and be considered in good standing.

A person possessed of some particular hobby can always find the time to indulge that hobby, whether it be dancing, the theatre, etc. Those who are genuinely interested in the study and practice of the Rosicrucian Philosophy, will have no difficulty in setting apart certain nights for attendance at Collegiate Convocations. Those who purpose to come only when it suits their convenience, or when they have nothing else to do, are advised to stay out of the Order. Its membership is limited and the Fraternity has no use for drones or social butterflies.

SICKNESS, OCCASIONAL URGENT BUSINESS ENGAGEMENTS, AND UNAVOIDABLY PROTRACTED ABSENCE FROM THE CITY are the only acceptable excuses for non-attendance. Habitual or chronic non-attendance renders such a member liable to temporary unaffiliation or dismissal from the Order without special notification.

The Fraternity receives all Neophytes in the kindest and broadest spirit of true brotherhood and fraternalism, and expects that each Neophyte will enter the ranks ready to extend such cordial sentiments to the Fraternity and each individual member in fullest measure, and take possible precaution against introducing inharmony in any form whatsoever.

All members are hereby requested to make it an invariable rule to see that each applicant is thoroughly informed as to these cardinal principles and requirements for admission as Neophytes. By observing this rule many lamentable mistakes may be avoided in the future.

𝔉𝔬𝔯𝔢𝔴𝔬𝔯𝔡

✠

THE Ancient Landmarks of the Fraternity given herewith, are those arranged by Fr. Johann Valentine Andreas from earlier relics, to which were appended a few new constructions. They were adopted and ratified by the Fraternity at Hamburg in 1614.

It is obvious that many of them are impossible of literal observance at the present day. Several of the Landmarks show unmistakably their adoption to have been caused by contemporaneous conditions which no longer exist, while the archaic construction of nearly all attests the antiquity with which they are surrounded.

It is to be understood, however, that so far as is practicable and possible, the Societas Rosicruciana In America is obligated to observe and maintain the intent, spirit, and purpose which inspired the original promulgation of these articles.

The Constitution of the Societas Rosicruciana In America and the By-Laws of Metropolitan College, S∴R∴I∴A∴, are given in accordance with the Revision adopted and authorized by the High Council and the College conjointly in 1919 and ordered done into print for the information of the Fraters.

Khei X⁰

The Ancient Landmarks

of the

Most Holy Order of the Ruby Rose and the Golden Cross.

As adopted by the Fraternity in the Year 1614.

Deut. 19-14   "*Thou shalt not remove thy neighbor's landmark which they of old time have set in thine inheritance, which thou shalt inherit in the land that the Lord thy God giveth thee to possess it.*"

Deut. 27-17   "*Cursed be he that removeth his neighbor's landmark. And all the people shall say, Amen.*"

Job. 24-1   "*Why, seeing times are not hidden from the Almighty, do they that know Him not see His days ?*"

2   "*Some remove the Landmarks; they violently take away flocks and feed thereof.*"

Prov. 22-28   "*Remove not the ancient landmark, which thy fathers have set.*"

23-10   "*Remove not the old landmarks, and enter not into the fields of the fatherless.*"

Isa. 19-19   "*In that day shall there be an altar to the Lord in the midst of the land of Egypt, and a pillar at the border thereof to the Lord.*"

20   "*And it shall be for a sign and for a witness unto the Lord of Hosts in the land of Egypt; for they shall cry unto the Lord because of the oppressors, and he shall send them a saviour and a great one, and he shall deliver them.*"

1   The Brotherhood shall not consist of more than 63 members.

2   The initiation of Catholics shall be allowed, and one member is prohibited to question another about his belief.

3   The ten years' office of the Rosicrucian Imperator shall be abolished and he shall be elected for life.

4   The Imperator shall keep the address of every member on his list, to enable them to help each other in case of necessity. A list of all names and birthplaces shall likewise be kept. The eldest brother shall always be Imperator. Two houses shall be erected at Nurenberg and Ancona for the periodical conventions.

5   If two or three brethren meet together, they shall not be empowered to elect a new member without the permission of the Imperator. Any such election shall be void.

6   The young apprentice or brother shall be obedient unto death to his master.

7   The brothers shall not eat together except on Sundays, but if they work together, they shall be allowed to live, eat, and drink in common.

8   It is prohibited for a father to elect his son or brother, unless he shall have proved him well. It is better to elect a stranger so as to prevent the Art becoming hereditary.

9   Although two or three of the brethren may be gathered together, they shall not permit anyone, whomsoever it may be, to make his pro-

fession to the Order unless he shall have previously taken part in the Practice, and has had full experience of all its workings, and has, moreover, an earnest desire to acquire the Art.

10   When one of the brethren intends to make an heir, such an one shall confess in one of the churches built at our expense, and afterwards shall remain about two years as an apprentice. During this probation he shall be made known to the Congregation, and the Imperator shall be informed of his name, country, profession, and origin, to enable him to despatch two or three members at the proper time with his seal to make the apprentice a brother.

11   When the brethren meet, they shall salute each other in the following manner:—The first shall say, **Ave Frater!** The second shall answer, **Roseae et Aureae.** Whereupon the first shall conclude with **Crucis.** After they have thus discovered their position, they shall say, one to another, "**Benedictus, Dominus Deus noster qui dedit nobis signum,**" and shall also uncover their seals, because if the name be falsified, the seal cannot.

12   It is commanded that every brother shall set to work after he has been accepted in our large houses, and has been endowed with the Stone (he receives always a sufficient portion to ensure his life for the space of sixty years). Before beginning he shall recommend himself to God, pledging himself not to use his secret Art to offend Him, to destroy or corrupt the empire, to become a tyrant through ambition or other causes, but always to appear ignorant, invariably asserting that the existence of such secret arts is only proclaimed by charlatans.

13   It is prohibited to make extracts from the secret writings, or to have them printed, without permission from the Congregation; also to sign them with the names or characters of any brother. Likewise, it is prohibited to print anything against the Art.

14   The brethren shall only be allowed to discourse of the Secret Art in a well closed room.

15   It is permitted for one brother to bestow the Stone upon another brother freely, for it shall not be said that this gift of God can be bought with a price.

16   It is not permissible to kneel before anyone, under any circumstances, unless that person be a member of the Order.

17   The brethren shall neither talk much nor marry. Yet it shall be lawful for a member to take a wife if he very much desire it, but he shall live with her in a philosophical mind. He shall not allow his wife to practice overmuch with the younger brethren. With the older members she shall be permitted to practice, and he shall value the honour of his children as his own.

18   The brethren shall refrain from stirring up discord and hatred among men. They shall not discourse of the soul, whether in human beings, animals, or plants, nor of any other subject which, however natural to themselves, may appear miraculous to the common understanding. Such discourse can easily lead to their discovery, (as occurred at Rome in the year 1620). But if the brethren be alone they may speak of these secret things.

19   It is forbidden to give any portion of the Stone to a woman in labour, as she would be brought to bed prematurely.

20   The Stone shall not be used at the chase.

21 No person having the Stone in his possession shall ask a favor of any one.

22 It is not allowable to manufacture pearls or precious stones larger than the natural size.

23 It is forbidden (under penalty of punishment in one of our large houses) that anyone shall make public the sacred and secret matter, or any manipulation, coagulation, or solution thereof.

24 Because it may happen that several brethren are present together in the same town, it is advised, but not commanded, that on Whitsunday any brother shall go to that end of the town which is situated towards sunrise and shall hang up a green cross if he be a Rosicrucian, and a red one if he be a brother of the Golden Cross. Afterwards, such a brother shall tarry in the vicinity till sunset, to see if another brother shall come and hang up his cross also, when they shall salute after the usual manner, make themselves mutually acquainted and subsequently inform the Imperator of their meeting.

25 The Imperator shall every ten years change his abode, name, and surname. Should he think it needful, he may do so at shorter periods, the brethren to be informed with all possible secrecy.

26 It is commanded that each brother, after his initiation into the Order, shall change his name and surname and alter his years with the Stone. Likewise, should he travel from one country to another, he shall change his name to prevent recognition.

27 No brother shall remain longer than ten years out of his own country, and whenever he departs into another he shall give notice of his destination, and of the name he has adopted.

28 No brother shall begin to work until he has been one year in the town where he is residing, and has made the acquaintance of its inhabitants. He shall have no acquaintance with the "professores ignorantes."

29 No brother shall dare to reveal his treasures, either of gold or of silver, to any person whomsoever; he shall be particularly careful with members of religious societies, two of our brethren having been lost, (anno 1641,) thereby. No member of any such society shall be accepted upon any pretence whatever.

30 While working, the brethren shall select persons of years as servants in preference to the young.

31 When the brethren wish to renew themselves, they must, in the first place, travel through another kingdom, and after their renovation is accomplished, must remain absent from their former abode.

32 When brethren dine together, the host, in accordance with the conditions already laid down, shall endeavor to instruct his guests as much as possible.

33 The brethren shall assemble in our great houses as frequently as possible, and shall communicate one to another the name and abode of the Imperator.

34 The brethren in their travels shall have no connection or conversation with women, but shall choose one or two friends, generally not of the Order.

35 When the brethren intend to leave any place, they shall divulge their destination to no one, neither shall they sell anything which they cannot carry away, but shall direct their landlord to divide it among the poor, if they do not return in six weeks.

36   A brother who is travelling shall carry nothing in oil, but only in the form of powder in the first projection, which shall be enclosed in a metallic box having a metal stopper.

37   No brother should carry any written description of the Art about him, but should he do so, it must be written in an enigmatical manner.

38   Brethren who travel, or take any active part in the world, shall not eat if invited by any man to his table unless their host has first tasted the food. If this be not possible, they shall take in the morning, before leaving home, one grain of our medicine in the sixth projection, after which they can eat without fear, but both in eating and drinking they shall be moderate.

39   No brother shall give the Stone in the sixth projection to strangers, but only to sick brethren.

40   If a brother who is at work with anyone, be questioned as to his position, he shall say that he is a novice and very ignorant.

41   Should a brother desire to work, he shall only employ an apprentice in default of securing the help of a brother, and shall be careful that such an apprentice is not present at all his operations.

42   No married man shall be eligible for initiation as a brother, and in case any brother seeks to appoint an heir, he shall choose some one unencumbered by many friends. If he have friends he must take a special oath to communicate the secrets to none, under penalty of punishment by the Imperator.

43   The brethren may take as an apprentice anyone they have chosen for their heir, provided he be ten years old. Let the person make profession. When the permission of the Imperator is obtained, whereby anybody is really accepted as a member, he can be constituted heir.

44   It is commanded that any brother who by any accident has been discovered by any prince, shall sooner die than initiate him into the secret; and all the other brethren, including the Imperator, shall be obliged to venture their lives for his liberation. If, by misfortune, the prince remain obstinate, and the brother dies to preserve the secret, he shall be declared a martyr, a relative shall be received in his place, and a monument with secret inscriptions shall be erected in his honour.

45   It is commanded that a new brother can only be received into the Order in one of the churches built at our expense, and in the presence of six brethren. It is necessary to instruct him for three months, and to provide him with all things needful. Afterwards he must receive the sign of Peace, a palm branch, and three kisses, with the words—"Dear brother, we command you to be silent." After this, he must kneel before the Imperator in a special dress, with an assistant on either side, the one being his magister, and the other a brother. He shall then say—"I, N. N., swear by the eternal and living God, not to make known the secret which has been communicated to me (here he uplifts two fingers) to any human being, but to preserve it in concealment under the natural seal all the days of my life; likewise to keep secret all things connected therewith as far as they may be made known to me; likewise to discover nothing concerning the position of our brotherhood, neither the name, surname, or abode of our Imperator, nor to shew the Stone to anyone; all which I promise to preserve eternally in silence, by peril of my life, as God and His Word may help me."

Afterwards his magister cuts seven tufts of hair from his head and seals them up in seven papers, writing on each the name and surname of the new brother, and giving them to the Imperator to keep. The next day the brethren proceed to the residence of the new brother, and eat therein without speaking or saluting one another. When they go away, however, they must say, "Frater Aureae (vel Roseae) Crucis, Deus sit tecum cum perpetuo silentio Deo promisso et nostrae sanctae congregationi." This is done three days in succession.

46   When these three days are passed, they shall give some gifts to the poor, according to their intention and discretion.

47   It is forbidden to tarry in our houses longer than two months together.

48   After a certain time the brethren shall be on a more familiar footing with the new brother, and shall instruct him as much as possible.

49   No brother need perform more than three projections while he stays at our large house, because there are certain operations that belong to the magisters.

50   The brethren shall be called, in their conversation with each other, by the name they received at their reception.

51   In presence of strangers they shall be called by their ordinary names.

52   The new brother shall invariably receive the name of the brother then last deceased; and all the brethren shall be obedient to these rules when they have been accepted by the Order, and have taken the oath of fidelity in the name of the Lord Jesus Christ.

53   In our smaller houses the magister shall not seek to exalt himself above the brethren.

54   In travelling from one country to another no brother shall carry any other means of defence than our Stone, in the sixth projection. He shall offer his own life before that of another, nor shall he take any life wantonly.

55   None of the brethren shall be constrained to dress outwardly, other than according to the habit of the country. In our great houses each shall be properly gowned and hooded according to custom ordained by the magisters, with bare feet and arms.

56   Every year, upon the day C the brethren shall meet together at the House of the Sancti Spiritus, or write the cause of such necessary absence.

57   Every brother shall look about him for a worthy person who, after his decease, might succeed him.

58   The word and letters R. C. shall be the seal, mark and character of the Order and brethren.

59   The Fraternity shall remain secret for one hundred years.

60   It is beyond the power of any brother to make changes or innovations in the essentials of our Rituals, Art or Operations.

61   No brother shall wear any outward sign, symbol, token, or badge of membership in the Order.

The Constitution

of the

Society of Rosicrucians, Incorporated,

and known as the

Societas Rosicruciana In America.

According to the Revision of 1919, and effective January 1st, 1920.

ARTICLE I.

The High Council.

Name and Object

Section 1. The name of this body is "The High Council of the Most Holy Order of the Ruby Rose and the Golden Cross."

Its Object is to Correlate Religion, Science and Philosophy; Promote the Study and Teaching of Moral Philosophy and Ethical Principles, and the Exploration of the Archaeological, Historical and Traditional subjects of Rosicrucianism, Freemasonry, Druidism and other arcane organizations. Its Practice is the Exposition and Promulgation of the Rosicrucian Art to Duly Qualified Initiates in the United States of America, and elsewhere, in full conformity with the Ancient Landmarks of the Rosicrucian Fraternity.

Provides for Ecclesiastic, Scientific and Philosophic Bodies

This High Council is Incorporated under three different classifications;

> As a Church—for the proper Ministration of the Sacraments and Doctrinal Exposition of the Religious Phase of Rosicrucian Teachings.
>
> As an Academic Institution for the Promotion of Scientific Research, and
>
> As a Fraternity for the practical Exposition of the Philosophy of the Origin, Evolution, Destiny and Brotherhood of Man.

In its Incorporation under these three classifications it becomes the

> SACRED COLLEGE, of the Ecclesiae Rosicrucianae Catholicae, (Rosicrucian Catholic Church; Incorporated).
>
> FACULTY, of the College of Scientific Research, Incorporated.
>
> HIGH COUNCIL of the Societas Rosicruciana in America (Society of Rosicrucians, Incorporated.)

Jurisdiction

Section 2. This High Council holds jurisdiction as the Sovereign Source of the Rosicrucian Art, throughout the United States of America and its possessions, and in such other countries as are not occupied by any legitimate Rosicrucian Body actually engaged in the practice of the Rosicrucian Art.

Clandestine Bodies

No organization claiming to be Rosicrucian shall be considered regular which does not operate under Charter or Dispensation from this High Council or from some Grand

Body of competent jurisdiction in affiliation with this High Council. Such bodies are held by this High Council to be clandestine and no member of the Societas Rosicruciana In America may hold Rosicrucian intercourse with any such body or the members thereof.

Of Whom Composed

Section 3. This High Council is composed of holders of Ninth Degree certificates, which shall be awarded under the conditions specified in Section 6 of this Constitution; but no one may be a member of this High Council who is not at the same time a member in good standing of a Subordinate College of the Societas Rosicruciana In America, and a Master Mason in good standing in a regularly constituted Lodge of Free and Accepted Masons hailing from a jurisdiction which is in affiliation with the Grand Lodge of Free and Accepted Masons of the State of New York, and loss of such good standing in College or Lodge automatically forfeits membership in this High Council.

Consistories

Section 4. Stated Consistories of this High Council shall be held as follows: Annually, on a date nearest approaching the Autumnal Equinox, for the conferring of the Eighth Degree; annually, on a date nearest approaching the Vernal Equinox, for the conferring of the Ninth Degree; annually, on the third Friday in December, for the purpose of receiving reports of officers concerning the progress of the Order; and at such other times for the transaction of business as the Magi may direct.

Interim Powers

Section 5. During the interim between Consistories, full power to transact all business of this High Council is vested in the Magi, acting in concert with the Secretary-General and Treasurer-General.

8th and 9th Degrees

Section 6. (a) The Eighth and Ninth Degrees are instructive, propagandive, and executive in their functions. The Eighth Degree confers the rank of Provincial Magus, and the Ninth Degree that of Lay Priesthood, upon recipients.

(b) By unanimous vote of the High Council, any frater may be designated to receive the Eighth Degree who is a member in good standing of his Subordinate College and who can satisfy the High Council, by oral and written examinations under conditions to be prescribed from time to time by the Magi, that he has advanced along the pathway of interior illumination and intellectual progress, and that he is able and willing to work for the good of the Order under instruction from the High Council.

(c) An Eighth Degree member, on making application and receiving the unanimous vote of the High Council, may qualify for the Ninth Degree by passing such oral and written examinations as may be prescribed by the Magi; by demonstrating psychic power in one or more phases; and by subscribing to the following declaration at the time application for the degree is made:

"I do solemnly declare upon my honor as a Rosicrucian that if elevated to the rank of Lay Priesthood through the conferring upon me of the Ninth Degree of the Ancient Rite, I will from thenceforth devote the remainder of my life, insofar as I may do so without detriment to my daily bread, to teaching and spreading the work of the Order, whenever

possible; that I will place this work above all other obligations, serious illness or urgent business alone excepted;
and that I will endeavor so to comport myself in the office
of Lay Priesthood as to reflect credit upon myself and honor
upon this Ancient Fraternity. In the Name of the S∴S∴.
Amen."

(d) It is herein specifically stated that the duties,
privileges and prerogatives of Eighth and Ninth Degree
Members shall be as follows:

Privileges of 8th and 9th Degree Members

EIGHTH AND NINTH DEGREE MEMBERS may act as
Deputies of this High Council, conduct the organization of
Subordinate Colleges and the Institution thereof under
Warrant from this High Council, preside over the Election
and Installation of Officers of Subordinate Colleges, exercise
any of the functions of the same upon request, and receive
the honors due them as Representatives from this High
Council when visiting Subordinate Colleges. Ninth Degree
members shall be eligible to election in the High Council
when vacancies therein occur.

NINTH DEGREE MEMBERS may assist at Ceremonial
Consistories of this High Council and in the Rite of Lay
Ordination when requested, and exercise all the preroga-
tives pertaining to the Office of Lay Priesthood and the
Rank of Prince Chief Adept.

(e) Initiation into the Eighth and Ninth Degrees does
not and shall not confer membership in the High Council,
S∴R∴I∴A∴. Said Membership shall be by nomination
by the Imperator, subject to confirmation by the Magi.

Officers

Section 7. The Officers of this High Council shall be
thirteen in number as follows:

13 Supreme Magus
(*Imperator*)

1 Senior Magus
(*Praemonstrator*)
2 Junior Magus
(*Cancellarius and
Treasurer General*)
3 Secretary-General
4 Celebrant
5 Primus Ancient
(*Acolyte*)
6 Chancellor

7 Secundus Ancient
(*Conductor of Novices*)
8 Tertius Ancient
(*Guardian of the Caverns*)
9 Quartus Ancient
(*Herald*)
0 Quintus Ancient
(*Orator*)
1 Sextus Ancient
(*Medallist*)
12 Septimus Ancient
(*Master of Ceremonies*)

Masonic Requirements

The Three Magi must be 32nd Degree Masons, and
members in good standing of some Consistory of the
A∴A∴S∴R∴. in affiliation with that of the Mother Council
of the Southern Jurisdiction at Washington, D. C., and must
also be members in good standing of a Regular Chapter
of Royal Arch Masons.

These Officers shall correlate with the Ecclesiastical Officers in accordance with the Canons of the Ecclesiae Rosi-
crucianae Catholicae. They shall also correlate with the
Officers of the Faculty of the College of Scientific Research.

How Chosen

Section 8. The offices of Senior and Junior Magi, Secretary-General and Treasurer-General, are elective; that of
Supreme Magus is filled in the manner described in Section
18; and all other officers are appointed by the Supreme
Magus.

Terms of Office

Section 9.   The office of Imperator is for life.   The terms of office of all other officers shall be for one year.

Duties

Section 10.   The duties of the officers of this High Council and of Subordinate Bodies shall be in accordance with the Rituals, Rubrics and Ancient Landmarks of the Rosicrucian Fraternity.

Imperator

Section 11.   The Imperator is vested with all the rights, privileges, powers and immunities conferred on his office by the Landmarks.   To him full allegiance must be given by all members of the Societas Rosicruciana In America as the Chief Executive of the Brotherhood in this country.

Praemonstrator

Section 12.   The Praemonstrator has full direction of the Propaganda of the Most Holy Order of the Ruby Rose and the Golden Cross, and the extension of the same throughout the territory under the jurisdiction of this High Council.   He is also charged with the Esoteric Correspondence of the Order.   He is vested with Plenary Powers of Authority to act in the absence of the Imperator, or, in the event of the Transition of the Imperator, until the successor to the same has been duly Confirmed and Proclaimed.

Cancellarius

Section 13.   The Cancellarius is the Custodian of the Work.   It is his duty to see that proper instruction is given to Subordinate Colleges in the rendition of the Rituals.   He may in his discretion require any officer of a Subordinate College to demonstrate suitable proficiency in his part before permitting him to perform the same; and from the Cancellarius' decision in matters of Ritual there is no appeal except to the Imperator.

The Cancellarius is also the custodian of the records, archives, properties, etc., of this High Council.

Secretary-General

Section 14.   The Secretary-General shall conduct the Exoteric Correspondence of the Order under the direction of the Imperator; record the transactions of this High Council and its Congegations; keep a registry of members of this High Council and of Subordinate Colleges, together with their esoteric names, mottoes and symbols; receive and safely file all documents of the High Council; sign and certify all instruments issued by authority of the High Council; receive and keep a proper account of all moneys of the High Council and pay the same without delay to the Treasurer-General; render a complete account of the transactions of his office at the annual Consistory in December, and perform such other duties as may be imposed upon him by the High Council.

Treasurer-General

Section 15.   It shall be the duty of the Treasurer-General to receive from the Secretary-General all moneys belonging to the High Council, giving his receipt therefor, and to pay out the same upon warrants duly signed by the Imperator and countersigned by the Secretary-General; to render a just and true account of the financial condition of the High Council at the Annual Consistory in December and at other times when called upon.

Vacancies

Section 16.   Vacancies in the appointive offices, occurring through death, resignation or otherwise, may be filled at any time by the Imperator.   Vacancies in the elective offices shall be filled by ballot at the Annual Meeting of the Corporate Body, but they may be temporarily filled by appointment from the Imperator.

Removal

Section 17. An appointive officer may be removed at any time by the Imperator if in his judgment such action will promote the good and welfare of the Order; and from his decision there is no appeal.

Imperator, How Chosen

Section 18. Within six months after taking office, the Imperator shall privately choose his successor, whose name he shall place in a sealed envelope and deliver the same to the custody of the Secretary-General. Upon the transition of the Imperator, such envelope shall be opened by the Secretary-General in the presence of the High Council in full Consistory assembled. Should the name of the frater chosen be unanimously approved by the High Council, he shall be declared elected, and installed in due form. Should the choice be disapproved, the High Council shall proceed by ballot to choose an Imperator from among their number, such choice requiring a three-fourths vote of those present. In the interim between the transition of the Imperator and the installation of his successor, the duties of Imperator shall be performed by the Praemonstrator.

Corporate Body

Section 19. The Societas Rosicruciana In America having been incorporated under the laws of the State of New York as the Society of Rosicrucians, the officers of the Incorporated Body shall consist of a President, Treasurer, Secretary and four directors. These seven shall constitute the Board of Trustees of the Corporate Body.

Officers

Section 20. The following officers of the High Council are officers and directors of the Corporate Body.

Imperator	President
Praemonstrator	Director
Cancellarius	Treasurer
Celebrant	Director
Secretary-General	Secretary
Primus Ancient	Director
Conductor of Novices	Director

Duties

Section 21. The duties of the President, Secretary, Treasurer and Directors of the Corporate Body shall be those usually devolving upon such officers. Four shall constitute a quorum to do business.

Annual Meetings

Section 22. The Annual Meeting of the Corporate Body shall be held on the third Friday in December of each year.

Congregations

Section 23. (a) The executive work of the Order in its various branches is divided for convenient operation into Congregations under the direction of the Imperator. These Congregations shall include the following:

1—Congregation of the Propaganda.
2—Congregation of Masonic Affairs.
3—Congregation of the Inquisition.
4—Congregation of Ecclesiastical Activities.
5—Congregation of Ritual and Ceremonial.
6—Congregation of Healing.
    and such other Congregations as may be found necessary.

(b) The Imperator may appoint a Prefect for each Congregation. The Secretary-General is ex-officio secretary of all Congregations.

College of Ancients

Section 24. The educational work of the Order is the province of the Faculty of the College of Scientific Research.

ARTICLE II.

Subordinate Colleges.

How Chartered

Section 25. A Subordinate College of the Societas Rosicruciana In America may be organized by twelve or more fraters, or members of the Congregation of the Outer, upon due petition to the High Council. Such petition shall be accompanied by a charter fee of twenty-five dollars.

A Charter can be granted only upon vote of the High Council in Consistory assembled, and shall bear upon its face the Great Seal of this High Council and the signatures of the Imperator, Praemonstrator, Cancellarius, Secretary-General, Treasurer-General and Primus Ancient.

Collegiate Officers

Section 26. The officers of a Subordinate College are sixteen in number, as follows:

Worshipful Adept	Primus Ancient
Celebrant	Secundus Ancient
Suffragan	Tertius Ancient
Treasurer	Quartus Ancient
Secretary	Organist
Conductor of Novices	First Herald
Acolyte	Second Herald
Guardian of the Caverns	Medallist

How Chosen

Section 27. The Worshipful Adept, Celebrant, Suffragan, Secretary, Treasurer (and Trustees when the same are deemed necessary) are elective; all others are appointed by the Worshipful Adept.

Convocations

Section 28. Stated convocations of a Subordinate College shall be held at the regular intervals provided by its by-laws. Special convocations may be called at any time by the Worshipful Adept on due and timely notice to the members. An Annual Memorial Convocation for the commemoration of members who have passed to the Higher Life is mandatory for each Subordinate College.

The reports of annual convocations of all Colleges for election of officers, receiving reports, etc., must be completed not later than December 1st of each year, and list of officers elected shall be certified to the Secretary-General within two weeks thereafter.

No business, reading of minutes, etc., shall be transacted at a Regular Convocation of any College of the Order. Only reports under the heading of "Sickness and Distress" and the necessary presentation of Applications for Membership with possible balloting thereon shall be permitted. No incidents not in harmony with the religious and philosophical nature of the Convocations shall be allowed. All business matters are to be discussed at Regular Quarterly Business Meetings of the College which shall be held at the call of the Adept during the year.

Forfeiture

Section 29. The Charter of a Subordinate College may be forfeited and revoked at any time at the discretion of this High Council for failure to observe true allegiance and obedience to its rules, regulations, edicts, by-laws and Constitution, failure to maintain collegiate work and convocations, or refusal to promulgate the principles of our Art and Operations in accordance with the Landmarks of the Institution or the Intent of its Founders.

Per Capita
Tax

Section 30. For the support and maintenance of this High Council a tax of $1 per capita shall be levied on all Subordinate Colleges whose annual dues do not exceed $6.00; a special pro rata tax may be levied upon all Subordinate Colleges whose annual dues exceed this amount.

Audit

Section 31. All secretaries of Subordinate Colleges are required to have their books closed for audit on or before the thirtieth (30th) day of November in each year; and the tax levied by the High Council shall be computed upon the basis of such membership as shall be recorded at the time of closing the books; and each secretary shall make his returns to this High Council not later than the tenth (10th) day of December following. A certificate of satisfactory audit by the local auditing committee shall accompany the returns in every case.

ARTICLE III.

Membership—Applications.

Who May
Be Members

Section 32. Membership in this Order is open to men and women of good character who have signified their desire to enter upon a study of Nature's laws, as revealed thru the occult wisdom of the Fraternity, and who are not debarred by any provision contained in the official publications of this High Council.

Applications,
How
Presented

Section 33. Applications for membership in a subordinate College must be presented at a stated convocation and be referred to a Congregation of Examiners for investigation. At least two weeks must elapse after an application is presented, before the same can be acted upon. Each application shall invariably be accompanied by a photograph of the applicant.

Tax

Section 34. It shall be the duty of the Secretary of each Subordinate College, immediately upon receiving an application for memberhip, to make a copy of the name, address, time and place of birth of the applicant and send the same to the Secretary-General, accompanied by a fee of fifty cents for each application; upon the receipt of which, the Secretary-General, if he approve the application, will forward to the local secretary a set of membership cards, properly filled out for each candidate; and no action may be taken by a Subordinate College on such application until it shall have been approved by the Secretary-General.

Approval of
Application

Section 35. The Secretary-General is authorized to approve all such applications as come within his sphere of limitations designated as follows:

1.—If the applicant's name is not already on the list of any Subordinate College.

2.—If the applicant has not been previously rejected by a Subordinate College.

3.—If the applicant has not been unaffiliated or dishonorably discharged from any Subordinate College.

4.—If the applicant is not a member of a body held to be clandestine or irregular by this High Council.

Should any question arise as to the moral fitness or other qualifications of the applicant, the Secretary-General shall before taking action thereon make a suitable investigation or cause the same to be done, reporting the facts and his decision to the High Council at its next Consistory.

The Secretary of each Subordinate College is required to notify the Secretary-General of the action taken on all applications, which must be transmitted to him for filing in the archives of this High Council.

Certificates

Section 36. The issuance of membership certificates is the exclusive province of this High Council, and all such documents must issue through the office of the Secretary-General.

The use of certificates is mandatory for the following degrees: Neophyte, 0°-0°, and Adeptus Exemptus, 7°-4°.

Adeptus Exemptus

Section 37. Certificates of recognition on the Seventh Degree, Adeptus Exemptus, shall be issued only by he Secretary-General upon receipt of a voucher, for each certificate to be issued, from the secretary of the Subordinate College; such voucher to be signed by the three major officers of the College. Each certificate issued shall be signed by the Imperator and the Secretary-General, and countersigned by the Worshipful Adept and Secretary of the Subordinate College, and shall bear, in the places provided therefor, the black seal of the Subordinate College and the plain seal of this High Council.

ARTICLE IV.

Degrees—Fees.

Authority to Confer

Section 38. Subordinate Colleges are authorized to confer the following degrees: Neophyte, 0°-0°; Zelator, 1°-10°; Theoricus, 2°-9°; Practicus, 3°-8°; Philosophus, 4°-7°; Adeptus Junior, 5°-6°; Adeptus Senior, 6°-5°; Adeptus Exemptus, 7°-4°.

Fee for Recognition

Section 39. The fee for Recognition in any College shall be not less than ten dollars, and out of this fee the sum of fifty cents must be sent to the Secretary-General under the provisions of Section 34. The Recognition fee may be remitted by a College in special circumstances, but these must be reported to the Secretary-General for his approval at the time application is made; and such remission shall not absolve the College from paying to the High Council the tax described in Section 34. The fee for the Eighth Degree shall be Ten (10) Dollars and the fee for the Ninth Degree shall be Ten (10) Dollars, due and payable on the receipt of each Degree.

(b)   The Degrees of the Grades shall not be conferred oftener than once per annum, and always in full ceremonial form.   This provision however does not include the Degree of Neophyte, 0°-0°, which is Probationary.

Collegiate
Garb

Section 40.   Subordinate Colleges shall make suitable provision for including in the Recognition fee a charge sufficient to cover the cost of a collegiate gown for the candidate, to be supplied to him for his exclusive use as soon after his initiation as possible.

The wearing of the collegiate garb at every convocation is mandatory.

ARTICLE V.

Discipline.

The
Landmarks

Section 41.   The discipline of this organization consists in the rigid observance of the Ancient Landmarks of the Order as they shall be from time to time recovered and explained.   The penalty for non-observance of such shall be determined by the rules laid down in the Book of Discipline.

Suspension

Section 42.   Subordinate Colleges may make such regulations as they see fit for the suspension and restoration of members; but no such provision shall infringe the power of this High Council to direct the name of any member to be stricken from the rolls without notice.

Allegiance

Section 43.   All meeting notices and publications of Subordinate Colleges, other than certificates of membership, shall bear the following Statement of Allegiance:

"........... College   acknowledges allegiance to the Magi and Officers of the High Council of the Societas Rosicruciana In America and Affiliated Councils, as the Sovereign Source of the Rosicrucian Art in the United States of America.   The House of the S∴S∴ of this Obedience is at present situate in the City of New York."

It is further ordered that the name "Societas Rosicruciana In America" shall in no case be written in abbreviated form in any Statement of Allegiance.

Publication

Section 44.   With the exception of such matter as is already printed, all published matter bearing the imprint of the Order shall bear only the secret pseudonyms of the fraters concerned; in no case shall the proper name of a frater be divulged, with the following exceptions; secretaries of Subordinate Colleges and the Secretary-General are empowered to use their own names in public or in print, as may be necessary to carry on the business of the Order. It is further forbidden to divulge the extent of the membership.

Dispensa-
tions

Section 45.   Dispensations for any legitimate purpose may be granted by the Imperator or the Magi, duly issued over the seal of this High Council and the signature of the Secretary-General.

The following dispensation is specifically stated:

"All fraters of this Order who are at the time of their Recognition members of a Masonic body of any rite, or who may subsequently become such, are hereby permitted to carry and use swords in accordance with the legitimate usage of their respective bodies."

Collegiate By-Laws

Section 46. Local by-laws in conformity with the spirit of the Order and its Ancient Landmarks may be adopted by any College, subject to ratification by this High Council.

Exponents' Certificates

Section 47. No frater shall presume to act as an official or recognized teacher, instructor or exponent of the Rosicrucian Philosophy, Art or Operations, History or Traditions, unless duly authorized thereto by this High Council. Such authorization shall be given only after strict examination of the frater desiring so to act, and shall be confirmed by the issuance of an Exponent's Certificate.

ARTICLE VI.

Amendments

Section 48. Amendments to this Constitution may be adopted by a two-thirds vote of the members present at a regular Consistory of the High Council, after due notice of the proposed amendments has been sent to all the members of the High Council at least ten days previous to the date of action.

The By-Laws
of
Metropolitan College, S.·.R.·.I.·.A.·.

As Revised and Amended to December 31st, 1919.

ARTICLE I.

Name and Object

Section 1. The name of this organization shall be "Metropolitan College, Societas Rosicruciana In America."

Section 2. The Object of this organization shall be the Study and Teaching of Rosicrucian Philosophy and Science, and the Conferring of the Rosicrucian Degrees from Neophyte to Adeptus Exemptus, inclusive in accordance with the Ancient Landmarks and Rituals promulgated by authority of the High Council of the Societas Rosicruciana In America.

ARTICLE II.

Allegiance

Section 1. This organization hereby acknowledges allegiance to the High Council of the Societas Rosicruciana In America, from which body it receives its Charter; the said Charter being granted to this College on the express condition that it may be revoked by the High Council at any time for failure to maintain the Ancient Landmarks and Rituals of the Order, or disobedience of the edicts, laws and regulations of the said High Council.

ARTICLE III.

Jurisdiction

Section 1. The jurisdiction of this College shall be the city of New York (State of New York) and vicinity.

ARTICLE IV.

Officers

Section 1. The elective officers of this College shall be:

1. Worshipful Adept
2. Celebrant
3. Suffragan
5. Treasurer
4. Secretary
6. Three Trustees

Section 2. It shall be the duty of the Worshipful Adept at the time of his installation to appoint a Conductor of Novices, Acolyte, Primus, Secundus, Tertius and Quartus Ancients, First and Second Heralds, Organist, Medallist and Guardian of the Caverns, whose duties shall correspond with their respective stations.

Section 3. The duties of all officers of this College shall be in accordance with the Rituals, Rubrics and Ancient Landmarks of the Rosicrucian Fraternity.

Section 4. There shall be three trustees elected by ballot to hold office for one, two and three years. At the expiration of the first year and each succeeding year thereafter, one trustee shall be elected for a term of three years.

Section 5. The Worshipful Adept, Celebrant and Suffragan shall constitute a Finance Committee with power to pass upon all bills, examine the books and accounts of the secretary and treasurer and report upon the same at the Annual Convocation and at such times as the College may direct.

ARTICLE V.

Meetings

Section 1. Stated convocations shall be held on the second and fourth Fridays of each month. Special convocations may be called at any time by the Worshipful Adept. Regular Quarterly Business Meetings shall be held in February, May, September and November.

Section 2. The Annual Meeting of this College for the election of officers and the transaction of such other business as may be hereafter prescribed, shall be held on the second convocation in November. Installation of officers shall take place at the second convocation in December.

ARTICLE VI.

Membership and Fees

Section 1. Membership in this College shall be open to men and women of good character who have manifested a desire to advance in esoteric knowledge.

Section 2. Applications for recognition shall be presented at a regular convocation and referred to a committee of three for investigation, which committee shall report at the next succeeding convocation unless further time be given.

Section 3. Each application shall be accompanied by a fee of ten dollars, which shall be applied as part payment for recognition if the candidate is accepted, but returned in case of rejection. Each application must also be accompanied by a photograph of the applicant.

Section 4. The fee for recognition shall be twenty-five dollars, payment of which must be completed at the time of recognition. This fee is to include the cost of a collegiate gown to be furnished to the candidate without further charge.

Section 5. Any candidate failing to appear for recognition within sixty days after being notified to do so shall forfeit the proposition fee and the election be declared void, unless a satisfactory reason for absence be given and the time extended by a majority vote of the College.

Section 6. The dues shall be ten dollars per annum, payable semi-annually or quarterly in advance.

ARTICLE VII.

Discipline

Section 1. The discipline of this College shall consist in the rigid observance of the Ancient Landmarks of the Order as they shall be from time to time explained and promulgated by the High Council. The penalty for non-observance of such shall be unaffiliation by this College, or in exceptional cases, such action as shall be prescribed by the High Council in accordance with the Ancient Usages of the Order.

ARTICLE VIII.

Suspension   Section 1.   Any member who shall fail to maintain collegiate standing by reason of protracted absence from its convocations, except for good cause, or by neglect or refusal to pay his dues for a period exceeding one year, shall upon a majority vote of those present at a regular convocation, be suspended from all privileges of membership and such action reported to the High Council; provided, that in all such cases a summons shall be sent to such member, under the seal of the College, giving thirty days' time for the member to appear and show cause why this action should not be taken.

Section 2.   Nothing in the foregoing section shall be held to infringe the power of this College to drop the name of any member from the roll, without notice, when ordered to do so by the High Council.

Section 3.   Any member who has been dropped from the roll for failure to maintain collegiate standing or for any other reason, may make application for reinstatement upon removing or healing the cause of his disability and such applicant for reinstatement, after being referred to the usual investigating committee, shall be balloted upon in the same way as a candidate seeking recognition; provided, however, that in the case of an unaffiliated member dropped under the provisions of Section 2, his application shall not be acted on until it has first received the approval of the Secretary-General.

ARTICLE IX.

Amendments   Amendments to these By-Laws may be adopted by a two-thirds vote of the members present at any convocation, after due notice of such proposed amendments has been sent to all members of the College at least one week prior to the convocation at which such action is to be taken.

Principles and Practice
for
Rosicrucians
By Khei.

To which are added the Rules, Duties, Secret Signs, Symbols, Jewels
and the Signs Referring to the Divine Child; reprinted from
"In the Pronaos of the Temple," by Dr. Franz Hartmann.

THE Congregation of the Outer in the Most Holy Order of the Ruby
Rose and the Golden Cross is composed of those registered affil-
iates, who, having subscribed their intention and desire to become
regularly initiated and recognized fraters and sorores of a just
and duly constituted College of the Order, are debarred from
immediate acceptance therein by virtue of being resident in a
town or city wherein no such College is, at the time, operative.

To those desirous of entering the Order, and found worthy of the same, the
Fraternity opens the Congregation of the Outer, membership in which implies
actual, progressive work towards ultimate acceptance into a regularly constituted College.

Where two or more persons are enrolled in the Congregation of the Outer
in the same locality, such persons will be put in fraternal communication with
each other, that by unity and co-operation the work may be progressed more
rapidly in that section.

All persons enrolled and accepted into the Congregation of the Outer are
expected, as a sine qua non of retaining membership in the same, to first make
themselves as thoroly acquainted with the purpose, principles, and work of the
Order as possible, and second, to use their utmost endeavors to promulgate
those principles among a carefully selected list of prospective members, until
the requisite number—twelve—has been attained; whereupon proper instructions for the organization and institution of a regular College in that section will
be sent from the High Council.

Members of the Congregation of the Outer will find herein a set of definite
principles and practices which they are to master fully and apply personally,
as a preparation for the more exclusively occult work which is given out only
in a College working in full ceremonial form under a Charter from the High
Council, in conformity with the Ancient Landmarks of the Fraternity.

Members of the Congregation of the Outer are known as Postulants. Members of a regular College are known as Fraters or Sorores, as the case may be.

Upon reading over the following pages, the Postulant who may be seeking
the weird or spectacular will undoubtedly be greatly disappointed. Curiosity
will be far from satisfied. The Rosicrucian Brotherhood does not offer spectacular or weird ceremonies, neither is it a spiritualistic organization, main-
taining seances, or encouraging or fostering so-called "fortune telling" in any
degree.

The "Occult" means simply the "hidden," and the Postulant in the Congregation of the Outer is regarded as one who is desirous of learning the innermost secrets of Nature.

As a pre-requisite to such knowledge, however, the Postulant must first of all begin the study of himself, for the extent of all knowledge he may gain will be measured absolutely by the knowledge he gains of his own self—and its attributes.

Consonant with this personal knowledge is the ability to exercise self-control, which ability is only to be gained by systematic adherence to definite principles based, not upon the fads and fancies of the day, but upon well demonstrated and attested rules which have been formulated solely thru actual practice by the initiates of many ages, and amply supported by the advancing science of the day.

The attainment of such self-control is positively the first step in the pathway of occult science—a science which embraces the whole range of human attainment and human knowledge; a science which leads us undeviatingly to the most exalted understanding of Infinity—of Divinity.

Mere reading of the following pages will not suffice. They are to be made a part of your intellectual working equipment, a groundwork for future development. Every separate principle is to be mentally and physically correlated with every other principle. Each principle affords an excellent subject for concentration and meditation. Each principle offers a distinct subject for accurate study.

For instance, under the heading of **Dietetics** the Postulant who desires to KNOW, will secure a good text book on physiology and master the entire scheme of the digestive, assimilative, and excretive processes, as well as understanding the table of food values.

The Postulant who desires to get the most out of concentration will master the contents of a good text book on psychology, understanding thereby the operations of the various systems and avenues of sense perception, the functions of the cerebro-spinal system, and the various optical and other sense illusions which so many credulous persons in their ignorance take for psychical or spiritualistic manifestations.

The Postulant who is studying the subject of **Rest** will also study both the physiology and psychology of sleep, consciousness, and especially the subject of the so-called "Twilight Sleep" which modern science has just entered upon but which has been fully known to the initiates of past ages.

Remember that Rosicrucianism is, above all things, occultism in its truest and deepest sense, but it is a form of occultism that provides no place for credulity, sentimentality, or seeking after the curious. It is based absolutely upon exact science. Perhaps it goes farther in some things than academic science is willing to concede, but the Society has enjoyed the pleasure for many ages, of witnessing the triumphs of its findings in their acceptance and confirmation by the exoteric science of the day.

Now a word as to the Order itself.

The time honored name of the Fraternity is: "The Most Holy Order of the Ruby Rose and the Golden Cross." For purely legal, as well as traditional purposes, it is incorporated (under the Laws of the State of New York) in this country as "The Society of Rosicrucians, Inc." New York State law prohibits the incorporation of any society under a name given in a foreign language. The legal name, therefore, is the one just given, which is always coupled, however, with the territorial name of the Society in Latin, "Societas Rosicruciana In America," following the custom of the various foreign Councils.

You can always identify a legitimate Rosicrucian body of this obedience in affiliation with the High Council by the use after its Collegiate name of the letters S.·.R.·.I.·.A.·., a formula which we rigidly protect by law. Thus the College at new York is known as "Metropolitan College, S.·.R.·.I.·.A.·.:" The High Council is not in fraternal affiliation with any other body in America claiming to be Rosicrucian, except the Temple of the Rosy Cross, nor does it recognize any other bodies to be such, altho it may fully and fraternally recognize the value of genuine occult work accomplished by many other organizations. With all genuine academic and humanitarian organizations, the S.·.R.·.I.·.A.·. is in complete harmony and concord, the stand enunciated above being purely one of legal position and traditional acceptance.

Every Postulant is required to supply himself with a copy of the standard text book of the Order, entitled "Rosicrucian Fundamentals," containing fourteen graded Instructions with questions.

The work of the Order may be classified under two distinct heads, viz.—its **Principles** and its **Practices.**

The Principles of the Order are contained in the following affirmations: We affirm—

The existence of One Infinite Intelligence, Omnific, Omniscient, and Omnipotent in its functions; from which we emanated as unconscious spirit substance, and to which we return as conscious, individualized entities.

We affirm—

The Incarnation of the Spirit, in visible form or Matter, to be for the purpose of Experience.

We affirm—

That all Life is Continuous, without Beginning and without Ending; Evolutional, in a constantly ascending scale of Progression.

We affirm—

That the Mortal may attain to the Knowledge of the Spiritual, while yet Incarnate.

And we affirm—

The Truth of Re-incarnation as a factor in the Soul's Evolutionary Progress, necessary as many times as may be required for the Assimilation of the Requisite Experience.

The acceptance of these cardinal principles of Rosicrucian doctrine is obligatory before you can be admitted as a Recognized or Initiated member of a regular College.

These principles are the motifs which your future work and study in the Order are to verify and demonstrate. In the advanced work of the second grade of the Order, laboratory research is required of each member. This does not mean that an elaborate laboratory is to be set up by each member, but it does mean that theory is to be supported by facts, only to be had by experimental demonstration; and full directions as to how this may be easily accomplished will be given when the appropriate time for each member to undertake it arrives.

The Practices of the Order relate to the study and personal application of a correct knowledge of

Concentration,	Dietetics,	Sexual Faculties,
Meditation,	Exercise,	Healing,
Contemplation,	Rest,	Cheerfulness,
Prayer,	Vitality,	Fasting,
	Individual Development.	

Concerning the first three practices, we shall not enter into a detailed explanation here, nor is it necessary for us to give explicit details as to their application, for this is completely set forth in a concise, readily understood manner, in "The Yoga Aphorisms of Patanjali" (Interpretation by William Q. Judge). This little book, pocket size for constant study and reference, may be had by sending to the Flame Press, Inc., 1429 Masonic Temple, 24th St., New York City, from whom also all books used or recommended by the Order may be had.

On the practice of Prayer, the Order takes what will seem to the orthodox the first radical step in a departure from traditional and current acceptance. The Frater who by systematic and open minded study comes face to face with his own soul, may experience somewhat of a shock to find that that soul has no knees. Likewise when he finds "God within," it will save much mental and spiritual energy for such an one to discard the ancient practice of trying to visualize an exterior Deity indefinitely evident, and supposed to pervade the cosmos, or localized by conjuring up a visualization of the Man on Golgotha.

The practice of Prayer, as inculcated by the Rosicrucian teaching, requires first of all the knowledge of the divinity of each individual human being; that every man and every woman is a God incarnate, and that each human being is an integral unit of the substance of the Absolute. Therefore the old theological concept of a God omnipresent, yet endowed with body, parts and passions, finds no place in our reverently advanced conceptions of His nature. Seek Divinity within yourself, not without.

Secondly, when engaged in the practice of Prayer, which should take place not once but many times daily (a momentary breathing can be made a prayer), all the avenues of sense perception should be closed to exterior impacts. Prayer is the establishment of perfect harmony or rapport between the Ego and its vehicles of expression. Seek not Divinity in some far off part of the cosmos. Imagine not that it is resident in some material heaven indefinitely located in the sky. Seek Divinity within **Yourself**—for it **is You** the Thinker— the Reader of this brochure. **You**—**Yourself**—are more than a mass of blood, bone and tissue. The real **You**, that operates through these substances, is the **Ego**, the spark of Divinity—the Holy Guardian Angel that is directing the progress and evolution of the various vehicles manifesting to the outer world in this or any given incarnation. It has been **You** from an eternity past. It will be **You** for eternity to come. Progressive, evolving—but—**Deathless.** You can no more get away from Divinity than you can divide yourself, separating one portion definitely from the other. Practice prayer, then, as the communion between your **Real Self** and your vehicles. Close your eyes, your ears, and your mouth. Shut out the exterior world, momentarily, or as long as you choose. Bring the troubles that confront you, the necessities apparent to you, the knowledge you seek, all matters pertaining to your visible vehicles—to **Yourself**. Address the God Within, and as your desire and its worth is, so shall your answer be.

The practice of proper Dietetics is one of great importance, and the position of the Order cannot be too accurately outlined. It may be a matter of surprise to many to learn that the Society is not avowedly a vegetarian organization. It endorses no special policy of eating or nutrition. The Rosicrucian who accomplishes the purpose of his membership will be able to eat what he will, and derive therefrom the maximum degree of benefit both in pleasure and nutritive value.

The Society does not agree that eating flesh foods converts a human stomach into a graveyard for dead animals, or any other such pleasant doctrine. Flesh foods have been a natural food for ages, and have been employed by the incarnating egos as material for the upbuilding of the physical body. The man who is engaged in vigorous physical labor requires a reasonable amount of flesh food to repair the loss of tissue. The man engaged in purely mental or intellectual pursuits needs **some** but less than in the previous instance. The man who seeks ardently the spiritual life still requires flesh food, but in a still lesser degree. Nature never intended human beings to be either more or less than—human beings, and the degree of saintliness purchased at the price of abnormal processes borders either upon the verge of faddism, selfishness, or mental abnormality.

The lower animals are indeed our younger brothers, but it is not necessary that they should breed excessively. They should be treated humanely and—when necessary—killed humanely, and the flesh of certain among them always has been, is, and will be for many cycles of evolution to come, valuable as body building food stuffs. The greatest men, warriors, statesmen, and philosophers have used flesh foods according to their needs. They **have not** been strict vegetarians.

At the same time, the Society **does** recommend a preponderance of vegetable and **Fruit Foods.** Each has its own proper place in the sphere of nutrition, as may be easily ascertained by reference to a standard table of food values. The Society **does** recommend and inculcate the desirability of minimizing the amount of flesh foods according to occupation, and the use to a very great degree of pure fruits and fruit juices. Immediately on arising, before swallowing, the mouth should be rinsed of the poisonous fluids which have accumulated therein during the night. Then a glass of hot water, sterilized (or boiled if sterilization is not convenient) should be taken, as hot as can be borne. At least two quarts of water should be consumed daily, hot if possible. Hot water is far more of a thirst quencher than cold water, and cold water is an absolute poison. Excessive use of sweets and highly seasoned foods should be eschewed, also use of coffee and tea to any abnormal degree. Used normally, one cup, not over strong, of either, at a meal, they can be considered beneficial. Alcoholics should not be used by one who expects to make satisfactory advances in occult science; not on temperance grounds, but solely because the unnaturally rapid internal combustion set up thereby, ensures a reaction that retards the desired progress, and unnatural stimuli are foreign to the purposes of Nature. Furthermore, one should remember that when trying to raise one's spiritual vibrations to a higher plane, it is suicidal to incorporate into one's vehicles the active, potent spirit of the corn or rye, thus lowering one's vibrations to the second life kingdom—the vegetable. This is retrogression. Pure, unfermented grape juice is ideal for those who would seek the spiritual life. In regard to the proper time for eating, the Society maintains that one should eat whenever one is hungry. There is a vast difference between **appetite** and **hunger.** The gourmand may have a constant appetite. Hunger, however, is a sure sign that the food already taken has been properly digested. Never eat to repletion. Eat whenever actually hungry, whether it be once or several times a day. Another thing, eat whatever you choose. The fact that you crave a certain food is an indication that the physical system demands just those chemical constituents that the food desired contains, and such food should be taken. It is not a good plan to eat heartily just before retiring, but an exceedingly light lunch is harmful to none and beneficial to many.

In the matter of foods, one rule is strongly insisted upon—abstinence from pork and veal.

At this point, it is well to devote a few words to the practice of systematic bathing.

A bath in tepid water daily is necessary to those who desire to make the most progress. This applies equally to women. The best medical advices will support our assertion that the traditional idea amongst women that a complete bath should not be taken while menstruating, is obsolete. Cold water should never be used at such times, but water lukewarm will not only not be harmful, but even beneficial. For those in good health, male or female, the warm bath should be followed by a cold or semi-cold spray and a quick rub, bringing on a vigorous reaction. This cold spray should of course be omitted by women during menstruation. Hot baths are an abhorrence, as they devitalize the system, as shown by the desire to sleep immediately afterwards.

For women, a warm or tepid douche once or twice daily is recommended, as preventing the accumulation of acrid and saline fluids, and keeping the female organism in a healthy, normal, and vigorous state.

For both sexes, the internal bath should be taken at least once every ten days. This can be done easily and without inconvenience by use of the new rubber seats and appliances, which can be had from any well equipped drug store. What is known as the "high enema" may also be used.

The entire length of the intestinal passages becomes lined with the accumulation of undigested food refuse, which prevents the digestive fluids from having free access to the intestinal convolutions, and in course of time becomes an interior obstruction to the processes of digestion to such an extent that many diseases may result therefrom. Keep the inside of your body as clean as the outside. It may be argued that this procedure was never used in olden times and our ancestors attained very great ages. Quite true, but civilization grows more and more complex with each succeeding generation, our lives, environments and habitat change and we must change our ideas as to hygiene accordingly. But in still older times, the ancients did use this method, and attained still greater age than did our more immediate ancestors. If you love life—keep clean—inside and out.

Another form of bathing which the Society has always insisted upon is known as the "Sunshine bath." This is simply exercise with intervals of rest in strong sunshine, absolutely nude. Mark this, however, the Society encourages no fantastic performances or procedure, nor does it countenance any sort of faddism. It does urge upon each member, the desirability of providing under suitable conditions for the frequent exposure of the entire body to the sunshine, and furthermore recommends that each member endeavor to arrange a part of his or her yearly or other vacation season in such a way that each can enjoy a portion of it under conditions which will allow of free, vigorous exercise followed by rest, in the open air, exposed to the sunshine. This practice was formerly carried by the Zoroastrians to a very high degree.

In the practice of Exercise, the Society provided for its proper recognition in a very practical manner during the earlier centuries. Then, in accordance with our Landsmarks, the members were not allowed to remain more than two months in a given country, with rest periods between intervals in some one of the Great Houses, as they were called. Now, however, such procedure is impossible. Proper and sufficient exercise should be taken daily in the open air, rain or shine, warm or cold, to the extent of a just noticeable feeling of fatigue. This of course applies to those leading a sedentary life. Those whose occupation keeps them in the open will gain all the access to pure air they will normally require. Walking is the very best and least tissue destroying exercise. Riding does one no special good except to bring the lungs in contact with good air. Exercise is required to create a better and more active blood circulation with consequent more vigorous assimilation of the vitalizing properties to be found in good fresh air.

In the matter of Rest, the Society teaches one to rest scientifically. This is as much a matter of practice as any of the others outlined herein. As stated in the introduction, the Postulant who desires to get the most out of his membership will provide himself with the best books to help him in his study. Halliburton's Physiology is excellent. In connection with the subject of rest, we also recommend "The Briefer Course in Physiology," by Prof. James, as helpful to a knowledge of the nervous system and its phenomena, and the importance thereto of proper rest conditions. It is during the state of sleep that our Etheric Body, the second of our vehicles, is actively at work restoring the depleted vitality and organic functions of the physical body, rebuilding the processes destroyed by the action of thought, movement, and general occupation of the day, and reconstructing and revitalizing the physical body in readiness for the ensuing day's activities. In connection with the subject of sleep, we strongly urge upon all members of the Society the advantages accruing from sleeping upon insulated beds. Glass fruit jar covers or glass receptacles such as are used on piano legs, answer nicely. Make sure that no bed clothing touches the floor or walls. Have the bed orientated so that you sleep with the head to the North.

This insulation keeps within the body the electric current it is constantly generating, and after a short while will ensure sound, perfect, dreamless sleep, and the feeling on awakening of being surcharged with vitality and vigor, and the desire to fairly leap from bed and begin actively the day's work. Sleeping with the head to the North ensures perfect harmony with the magnetic plane and materially assists the Etheric Body in its work of reconstruction. This harmony with the magnetic planes or meridians also acts powerfully in the development of personal magnetism, so valuable to every one in the various departments of life. You may experiment in the following manner: Have before you two vessels, one containing hot water, the other cold water, both strongly saline. Place the hands in each; then, after a moment, change hands, and you will feel the magnetic waves surge up the arms and across the shoulders. After sleeping in the manner described, you can readily keep track of your development in this particular sphere by noting the increase of strength in the magnetic wave.

Never lie down to rest for the purpose of getting a moment to think over something. At night, seek your bed with the sole idea predominant of complete oblivion, and, if your stomach is right, you should have no dreams.

Rest momentarily at intervals during the day, seeking some secluded nook or corner where you can close your eyes and "give up" completely, if even only for a few seconds. If this is impossible or inconvenient, rest at your desk, by placing the hand over the eyes, and dropping all thoughts of business or other occupation for a moment or two. This will give Nature a chance to restore equilibrium. If confronted by a special problem, do not keep working at it until your brain is on fire, your nerves upset, and your temper almost at the breaking point. Rest a moment; seek oblivion; and then go at it calmly and quietly, with firm resolve to master it, and the result achieved will be little short of miraculous.

In the last part of this section you will find a rule for daily practice for concentration. This it must be explained is not to be considered as preventive of the advice given above, to seek your bed with the sole thought of oblivion. On going directly to bed, seldom can one go immediately to sleep, especially if one leads an active mental or physical life.

When you retire, first carry out the practice therein enjoined, then fix the mind firmly on oblivion, at peace and harmony with the world. Rest means the readjustment of disturbed equilibrium, establishment of harmony and the proper conservation of one's energies, and should be practiced as "actively," as frequently and as systematically as one eats or exercises.

The subject of Vitality is closely allied to that of Exercise. It comprehends the restoration of lost vitality, the accumulation of fresh supplies of energy, the perfect oxidation of the blood, the renewal of nerve fiber and the maintenance of perfect poise and vigor. It also includes the development of personal magnetism.

The more exhaustive and detailed treatment of lost vitality and personal magnetism is given in the "Secret Work" pertaining to the later degrees in regular Collegiate Work."

The chief source from which we derive our vitality is the atmosphere. Among the ancient Greeks, the atmosphere was recognized as possessing besides its usually understood chemical constituents, an active force which they termed "glama." This same potency has been described by Bulwer Lytton as "Vril." It is known to modern science as "Ozone." It was known to the Hindus as "Akasa." Without going into a scientific explanation of this force, which belongs to the Secret Work and requires a careful reading on the subject of Physics and Chemistry, we will outline here a formula by which this **Solar Force** and **Energy** can be drawn systematically into the organism and utilized in the daily walks and works of life.

1. **Let the First Waking Thought be "Harmony."** Do not entertain another idea until that one has taken firm possession of your mind. Hold it thru the day. **Harmony With Nature, Harmony With Yourself. Harmony With Your Environment.**

2. Upon arising, go to your window, preferably one thru which the sun is streaming—**Without Clothing.** Admit as much fresh air as the season will permit. Stand erect; stretch every muscle of the body; then take a few moments of **Rythmic Breathing** as follows:

3. First—expel all carbonic acid gases from the lungs, so thoroly that the effects will be felt in the lower lobes.

4. Second—**Inhale, Retain,** and **Exhale** thru a given length of time, to wit:

> INHALE 6 Seconds
> RETAIN 3 Seconds
> EXHALE 6 Seconds.
> WAIT THREE SECONDS AND REPEAT.

One may count by seconds or by heart beats. Stretch the lungs to the fullest capacity during the inhalation. Breathe so deeply that the fresh air may be felt penetrating to the utmost extent of the lowre lobes of the lungs.

5. **Inhaling**—hold the thought that you inhale **Power** from the Universal Source of Power.

6. **Retaining**—hold the thought that you charge and vitalize your entire organism with this Power.

7. **Exhaling**—hold the thought that you send this Power forth to accomplish your desire.

8. At the close of the day, sum up the day's activities. Estimate the measure of your advance, or failure to advance in mental and physical power and harmony. Let the closing thought of the day be harmony.

9. Hold constantly the desire of mind, for a greater measure of comprehension of your latent powers, and of your relations to the worlds within and without you.

10. Whatever you do, above all, concentrate. Conserve your energy. Don't concentrate entirely on one thing alone, but concentrate vigorously **on one thing at a time**; whatever is before you.

To Sum Up: Charge the mind with **Harmony** at the instant of the waking state. Feed the Body, **Every Pore,** with sunshine and fresh air, not slighting three-fourths of the body in favor of the face and hands. Remember, every pore and cell has a right to nourishment as well. Cultivate the practice of complete nudity some portion of the day. You cannot expect the bodily organism to be at its best in vigor and vitality when three-fourths of it seldom gets more than the instant during robing and disrobing to come into contact with the vitalizing properties of the air. The value of cultivating the nude state is ably set forth at length by such an authority as Dr. Havelock Ellis, in his book "Sex in Relation to Society." Give every part of the surface of the body an opportunity to breathe. Then by **Rythmic Breathing** put these cells in **Harmonious Vibration** with all Nature about you. Do not go to sleep with your mind worried; charge it with this same harmony. Start the day clean, and you will be apt to have a good clean record at its close.

Making the above practices a part of your daily regime will soon vitalize and surcharge with vitality your entire organism, so that your accomplishments will be multiplied many fold and a sense of newness will enfold you that will give color to an otherwise colorless world and develop your potencies beyond your present power of imagination.

The **Sexual Faculties.** While this subject belongs again to the Secret Work we shall include enough data here to acquaint the Postulant fully with the position taken by the Society in regard to this subject and its teachings thereof. One of the first and most persistent subjects which come before the student of the occult, as well as before students in the domain of psychology, physiology, sociology and many kindred sciences, is sex. And probably no other subject has been so widely discussed, so vaguely treated and at the same time has been the subject of so many misconceptions, as this same subject of sex.

It is become the fad of certain occult bodies and the fetish of the prurient. We shall handle it respectfully, but as any other department in the domain of human science. The Societas Rosicruciana In America does not teach the idea of strict sexual continence. It does **not** regard the act of procreation as any sacrifice on the altar of humanity. Its attitude regarding sexual matters is in strict accordance with the best authorities on the subject, Ellis, Krafft-Ebing, Moll, etc., etc., and the findings of the best medical authorities, whose wide experience has given them ample opportunity of proving the accuracy of their position. Their views on the subject are the same as those held by this Order thruout many ages.

So far as the matter of reproduction or procreation is concerned, the Rosicrucian Neophyte does not progress very far in his studies without learning that the present modus is the third method that has obtained since man's evolution first began. First, the spiritual procreaion before man completed his mortal embodiments; then the hermaphroditic; now, the division into male and female and the consequent necessary union in the procreative act. The Neophyte also learns to look forward to the time when the evolutionary cycle shall have brought us to the original starting point—on a higher plane, when the hermaphroditic process will be again resumed, only to be followed by true spiritual procreation. But this is a matter of eons hence. At the present time the Order regards the existing modus of procreation as simply the natural process resulting from our evolutionary grades, and to be regulated simply by wisdom, economic and industrial conditions. It regards the parents as simply the avenues thru which an incarnating ego is enabled to emerge into the sphere of physical functions. It holds that the choice or option of the parents as to becoming such avenues of ingress should be controlled by their ability to bring in perfect physical organisms, fit to cope with the struggle for existence which confronts each one on its advent to our plane of being. This choice should also be controlled by the ability of the prospective parents to provide proper nourishment, material support, and proper equipment as to training and education for life's battle.

As to the use of the sexual powers for purposes other than strict intent to procreate, the Society also coincides with the views of eminent medical authorities, as to their beneficial results when not abused. This subject is fully treated of in the Secret Work of the Second Grade. As a distinct aid to female development after the age of adolescence, the relief of various nervous conditions, and the establishment of a perfect mental, physical and psychical rapprochement between the parties concerned, its beneficent usage is upheld. The Society holds that no union can approximate the ideal which is not based equally upon the three great principles of spiritual, intellectual and physical union, constantly maintained. With conventional marriage, occultism has nothing to do. Marriage is an outgrowth of certain sociological conditions, and while sacramental, should not be subject to the arbitrary disposition of either Church or State, the first often unscientific and the latter unspiritual in their respective viewpoints. In relation to this subject, the Postulant will do well to provide himself with a copy of Westermarck's "History of Human Marriage." It is not our province to discuss the subject of marriage here. We are concerned, as occultists, only with the natural viewpoint; that is, that the instincts which prompt the opposite sexes to approach each other are primitive in their origin, are not the creation of man or his system of ethics, and like the primitive instincts of the animal kingdom will seek a natural outlet; and that natural outlet must be provided and recognized.

We must also take occasion herein to state emphatically that this Society does not uphold what is commonly known as "promiscuity." With what relations may exist between the sexes as a result of the overpowering potencies of opposite magnetic polarities, we are not concerned, but to open the doors to the inrush of unbridled license, is absolutely foreign to the practice, philosophy, or ethics of this Fraternity.

The sexual relations between man and woman are matters of their own personal discretion and requirements, subject only to the exercise of wisdom, consideration, and the highest ethical essential attributes. Abuse of the sexual powers is condemned unreservedly.

The Postulant or Neophyte who seeks the highest spiritual development, will, without any formulated rule, soon discover that such can be best attained by the conservation of his or her energy, and in later communications it will be shown how the sexual powers can be transmuted into the highest intellectual and spiritual energy of a creative nature.

On one thing, however, the Society does take an unalterable stand. That is, the right of woman to control her own physical organism, and submit it to no man except by her own choice or her own free will. This Society does not relegate woman to the place which the ecclesiastical tyranny of Christianity has appointed her—that of an incubator. Glorious as motherhood is, when freely and deliberately desired, with all the environments as to adequate support and maintenance present, we believe that woman has her part to fill in the world's work and activity, outside the home as well as within. She has amply justified this position and the efforts of this Order ever have been and we believe, ever will be, toward the freeing of woman from her condition of serfdom, as man's chattel slave.

As an instance, however, of what may be accomplished by utilizing the sex powers for higher purposes, and creative powers rather than mere momentary sexual exaltation, the following practice may be undertaken by either sex.

At such times as sexual desire seems imperative, stand erect, muscles tense, place the hands palms down over the sex organs—partially or, better still, completely disrobed—and while doing so, concentrate on the thought: "I Will that this power ascend to higher regions—that it follow this path—I can feel it so doing," meanwhile drawing the hands up slowly on each side of the abdomen, following the natural curve of the body, until they stop over the nipples or mammary glands. Pause a moment until conscious of a distinct swelling of the breasts, a sensation of energy therein. Practice this on several occasions until the evidence of the upward surging of the vital powers is undoubted. Then, as a step farther, the next time it is practiced, bring the hands up to the throat, until it manifests in a distinct desire to speak with force and vigor. Third step—bring the hands completely up over the back and front brains, and you will become conscious of a power to create in the line of thought or mental process never before experienced. This practice is invaluable to the men or women who use their brains rather than their hands in the regular occupations of life.

Normal use of sex functions is by all means to be upheld. Faddism or abnormal usages are always to the unreservedly condemned. The day of the hermit and anchorite is past, and history does not record that much was ever accomplished by them. The day of the monastic life is also past, and the annals of time do not seem to record that vows of chastity produced either greater intellects, or a higher standard of purity. In fact, the greatest persecutions of advanced intellectual progress took place during the time when the monastic life held its greatest sway.

Under the head of Healing we comprehend the attitude of the Society regarding healing and medication. On this subect the Society takes a sane and solid stand, in line with the advanced ideas of medical authorities of the day. We do not endorse the use of drugs. Neither do we condemn them. The special mission of the Rosicrucian Fraternity is one of Healing, and this is dealt with in special Instructions given in our Colleges, relative to the formation of Healing Clinics. The best modern physicians use drugs the least. The Society regards disease as just what it is,—dis—ease; in other words, an imperfect equilibrium between the various constructive and destructive forces in the human body. If this disturbed equilibrium is brought about by unnatural methods of living, the best cure of all is to return to the natural method of living. The organism which is kept in the perfect harmony referred to a few pages back will seldom require medication.

More powerful than drugs, in all except injury to the bony framework and organic troubles, is the potent power of mind. By realizing that dis—ease is a disturbance of equilibrium, and so-called sickness an illusion of the senses, the power of mind can be brought to bear so potently that a restoration to perfect health quickly follows. In such recalcitrant cases as cannot accept this fact exterior medication is very properly applied, as it was never the intention of Nature that any of her children should suffer unnecessarily. As stated before, Healing forms a separate subject for study and finds its proper place in the work of the Order after the Postulant is duly initiated into a regular College, The same is also true of the previous subject—Sex.

At the beginning of a previous paragraph we stated that the Society did not endorse the use of drugs, neither did it condemn them. This requires elucidation. The Rosicrucian Fraternity does not approve of the use of mineral poisons as medicines, or the use of pharmaceutical preparations involving the use of the active factors of the poisonous venom of reptiles. That is a distinct reversion to the conditions of the "Dark Ages." On the other hand this Society has always recognized, and studied, the beneficial and healing virtues of certain vegetable preparations, wherein Nature gives to mankind in a form readily and beneficially assimilated, the marvelous curative potencies from her own great laboratory. It is and always has been, a part of the work of this Order to give to mankind those remedies which Nature approves and has had ready for it from the foundation of the world.

Cheerfulness. It would hardly seem that cheerfulness is a subject which requires regular practice, yet a little reflection will reveal that such is the case. Cheerfulness does not mean the ordinary moods of good nature which mark our daily lives. Supreme cheerfulness is a distinct art, a distinct acquirement. The Rosicrucian Order is a clerical order. It is not, however, a monastic Order. It imposes no gloomy vows of silence and unnatural conditions upon its members. On the contrary, Lytton records of its members that "they were generally distinguished for their extreme sociability." The Order distinctly requires its members to mix with the world at large, to dance, sing, play, and cultivate the sunny disposition to the greatest possible extent.

Knowing that every thing that is, is right, because its very existence is required even when apparently wrong, in order to pave the way for reconstruction on a higher plane, and realizing that wrong, or so-called sin is but misdirected good, the Rosicrucian always attempts first of all to see the good, the beautiful in life, manifesting under the most trying conditions so far as possible an unfailingly cheerful nature and disposition. This does not mean frivolity, or a life lived solely for one's own selfish, personal gratification; for such the

Order has no welcome. But it does mean that to the cheerful Rosicrucian, life will become such a harmony as to reflect within his or her own organism the eternal harmony of the spheres, and prove the very elixir of life to those who can accomplish it.

Fasting is a practice to which the Order attaches especial virtue, not when undertaken as a fad, or religious duty, but when undertaken as a rest for the interior bodily processes. It should not be prolonged, but some have found it advantageous to fast for from three days to a week, at intervals of two or three months. After fasting, the Postulant should eat sparingly and not rush to a full meal. It will be found that a fast prior to times when unusual spiritual exaltation or illumination is desired, will greatly advance the personal development. It may be said here, and could have been properly included under the head of diet, that the less one eats, the better. It is not the amount but the manner of eating which makes for correct nutrition. One can live on very little if one masticates thoroughly, until there is nothing left to masticate.

Cultivate a frugal appetite, and masticate what is eaten, thoroly; and you will find yourself much better physically, spiritually, and intellectually.

In regard to individual development, we will not enter deeply into the subject here, as each phase of development is fully treated in special lessons for Collegiate Initiates.

The Order does not encourage development for fortune telling or the gratification of curiosity. It does require persistent efforts to develop one's spiritual powers, especially the power of clairvoyance. The spiritual life without spiritual illumination and the power and privilege of seeing spiritual things is like the power of touch to the man who can neither see nor hear. Each member is, by virtue of membership in this Order, expected and required to exert all possible endeavor to the development of the purely spiritual faculties and powers.

So much for the Practices of the Order. It is often asked by prospective members, if they are required to give up membership in this or that Church, or if they will be required to resign from some special society or give up some work in which they may be engaged. To all such questions the Order answers unreservedly—No. It does positively require—the **Open Mind**.

The member of an orthodox church will soon find, however, that he will be quite willing to exchange conceptions based solely upon faith, for ideas based absolutely upon demonstrable fact. He will be glad to exchange his hazy and puzzled idea of the Nazarene for the true knowledge of the lofty character and standing of the Man Jesus, actuated by the Christ Princple, as an actual historic personage, and one still living amongst us. The member of a worthy society will find himself a better member of that society as a result of his membership in this Fraternity.

The Society places no inhibition upon any mode of development that its members may find in accord with their individual personalities and requirements. It does guide such development whenever permitted. If help is declined, the Society allows such a member to pursue his or her own course until the error is manifest, then starts such an one on the right path. No liberty of thought or action on the part of any member is encroached upon, and the Society is open to Catholic or Protestant alike. The Order has no political or radical affiliations whatever, neither is it in sympathy with the various anti-Catholic movements and other forms of religious prejudice and sectarian bitterness, usually founded upon ignorance.

The sole requirements for admission are: the desire to lead the higher spiritual life, to develop one's powers, potencies, and spiritual faculties and the acceptance of the Five Affirmations as a common working basis for all its students. It furthermore requires strict adherence and observance to the obligations of secrecy, assumed by each member before and upon acceptance and enrollment.

For your instruction we print herewith the **Rules, Duties, and Secret Signs of a Rosicrucian,** taken from the writings of the late Franz Hartmann, a noted Rosicrucian and philosopher, in his book "The Pronaos of the Temple." These Rules, Duties and Secret Signs will indicate to you the path you have assumed to follow, and it is not an easy one.

You are not left to struggle alone, however, for the Council in enrolling you in the Congregation of the Outer, has placed you within the sphere of its healing and strengthening vibrations, sent out twice daily, at twelve o'clock noon, Eastern Standard Time, and at 12 o'clock midnight. At such times, you are earnestly requested to hold yourself receptive to such vibrations and to concentrate upon the Council and the work of the Order, and thus receive the fullest measure of our esoteric aid and encouragement

ROSICRUCIAN RULES.

1. Love God above all.

To "love God" means to love wisdom and truth. We can love God in no other way than in being obedient to Divine law; and to enable us to exercise that obedience conscientiously requires knowledge of the law, which can only be gained by practice.

2. Devote your time to your spiritual advancement.

As the sun without leaving his place in the sky sends his rays upon the earth to shine upon the pure and the impure, and to illuminate even the most minute material objects with his light; likewise the spirit of man may send his mental rays into matter to obtain knowledge of all terrestrial things; but there is no need that the spirit should thereby lose its own divine self-consciousness, and be itself absorbed by the objects of its perception.

3. Be entirely unselfish.

Spiritual knowledge begins only where all sense of self ceases. Where the delusion which causes man to imagine himself to be a being separated and isolated from others ends, there he begins to realize his true state as an all-embracing universal and divine self-conscious power.

4. Be temperate, modest, energetic, and silent.

The door to the inner temple is called "Contentment"; but no animal can enter therein, only he who walks uprightly, being conscious of his true dignity as a human being. Without energy, nothing can be accomplished; and only in the silence, when all thoughts and desires are at rest, can the Divine harmonies penetrate to the internal ear.

5. Learn to know the origin of the Metals contained within thyself.

Ignorance is the cause of suffering. That which is material must be crucified and die, so that that which is spiritual may be resurrected and live.

6. Beware of quacks and pretenders.

He who claims to be in possession of knowledge knows nothing; only he through whom the Word of wisdom speaks is wise.

7. Live in constant adoration of the highest good.

The worm seeks for pleasure among abomination and filth; but the free eagle spreads his wings and rises up towards the sun.

8. Learn the theory before you attempt the practice.

He who travels with a trustworthy guide will be safer than he who refuses to profit by the experience of another.

9. **Exercise charity towards all beings.**

All beings are one in the spirit; divided from each other merely by the illusion of form. He who is charitable towards another form in which the universal One Life is manifest, saves suffering to his own self.

10. **Read the ancient books of wisdom.**

Books are to the unripe mind that which the mother's milk is to the nursling. We must receive drink from others until we have gained sufficient strength and experience to descend to the living fountain within ourselves, and to draw from there the water of truth.

11. **Try to understand their secret meaning.**

That which is external may be seen with the external eye; but that which is spiritual can only be seen with the eye of the spirit.

These are the eleven rules which ought to be followed by those who desire to enter the temple of the Rosy Cross; but the Rosicrucians have a twelfth rule, an **Arcanum**, in which great powers reside, but of which it is not lawful to speak. This Arcanum will be given to those who deserve it, and by its aid they will find light in the darkness, and a guiding hand through the labyrinth. This Arcanum is inexpressible in the language of mortals, and it can, therefore, only be communicated from **heart to heart**. There is no torture enough to extract it from the true Rosicrucian; for even if he were willing to reveal it, those who are unworthy of it are not capable of receiving it.

THE DUTIES OF A ROSICRUCIAN.

Those who are dead in the flesh will read the following with the external understanding; those who live in the spirit will see its internal meaning, and act accordingly.

The duties of a true Rosicrucian are:

1. **To alleviate suffering and to cure the sick without accepting any remuneration.**

The medicine which they give is more valuable than gold; it is of an invisible kind, and can be had for nothing everywhere.

2. **To adapt the style of their clothing to the costumes of the country wherein they reside for the time being.**

The clothing of the spirit is the form which he inhabits, and must be adapted to the conditions of the planet whereon he resides.

3. **To meet once a year in a certain place.**

Those who do not meet at that place, when their terrestrial career is over will have their names taken out of the book of life.

4. **Each member has to select a proper person to be his successor.**

Each man is himself the creator of that being whose personality he adopts on the next step on the ladder of evolution.

5. **The letters R. C. are the emblem of the Order.**

Those who have truly entered the Order will bear the marks upon their body, which cannot be mistaken by him who is capable of recognizing them.

6. **The existence of the Brotherhood is to be kept secret for one hundred years, beginning from the time when it was first established.**

Nor will the "hundred years" be over until man has awakened to the consciousness of his own divine nature.

THE SECRET SIGNS OF THE ROSICRUCIANS.

There are sixteen signs by which a member of the Order of the Rosicrucians may be known. He who possesses only a few of those signs is not a member of a very high degree, for the true Rosicrucian possesses them all.

1. The Rosicrucian is Patient.

His first and most important victory is the conquest of his own self. It is the victory over the LION, who has bitterly injured some of the best followers of the Rosy Cross. He is not to be vanquished by a fierce and inconsiderate attack made upon him; but he must be made to surrender to patience and fortitude. The true Rosicrucian tries to overcome his enemies by kindness, and those who hate him by gifts. He heaps not curses, but the burning fire of love upon their heads. He does not persecute his enemies with the sword, or with faggots, but he suffers the weeds to grow with the wheat until they are both matured, when they will be separated by Nature.

2. The Rosicrucian is Kind.

He never appears gloomy or melancholy, or with a scowl or sneer upon his face. He acts kindly and politely towards everybody, and is always ready to render assistance to others. Although he is different from the majority of other people, still he tries to accommodate himself to their ways, habits and manners, as much as his dignity will permit. He is, therefore, an agreeable companion, and knows how to converse with the rich as well as with the poor, and to move among all classes of society so as to command their respect; for he has conquered the BEAR of vulgarity.

3. The Rosicrucian knows no Envy.

Before he is accepted into the Order he must go through the terrible ordeal of cutting off the head of the SNAKE of envy; which is a very difficult labor, because the snake is sly, and easily hides itself in some corner. The true Rosicrucian is always content with his lot, knowing that it is such as he deserves it to be. He never worries about the advantages or riches which others possess, but wishes always the best to everybody. He knows that he will obtain all he deserves, and he cares not if any other person possesses more than he. He expects no favors, but he distributes his favors without any partiality.

4. The Rosicrucian does not Boast.

He knows that man is nothing but an instrument in the hands of GOD, and that he can accomplish nothing useful by his own will; the latter being nothing but the will of GOD perverted in man. To GOD he gives all the praise, and to that which is mortal he gives all the blame. He is in no inordinate haste to accomplish a thing, but he waits until he receives his orders from the Master who resides above and within. He is careful what he speaks about, and uses no unhallowed language.

5. The Rosicrucian is not Vain.

He proves thereby that there is something real in him, and that he is not like a blown-up bag filled with air. Applause or blame leaves him unaffected, nor does he feel aggrieved if he is contradicted or encounters contempt. He lives within himself, and enjoys the beauties of his own inner world, but he never desires to show off his possessions, nor to pride himself on any spiritual gifts which he may have attained. The greater his gifts, the greater will be his modesty, and the more will he be willing to be obedient to the law.

6. The Rosicrucian is not Disorderly.

He always strives to do his duty, and to act according to the order established by the law. He cares nothing for externalities, nor for ceremonies. The law is written within his heart, and therefore all his thoughts and acts are ruled by it. His respectability is not centered in his external appearance, but in his real being, which may be compared to a root from which all his actions spring. The interior beauty of his soul is reflected upon his exterior, and stamps all his acts with its seal; the light existing in his heart may be perceived in his eye by an expert; it is the mirror of the Divine image within.

7. The Rosicrucian is not Ambitious.

There is nothing more injurious to spiritual development and expansion of the soul than a narrow mind and a selfish character. The true Rosicrucian always cares much more for the welfare of others than for his own. He has no private or personal interest to defend or foster. He always seeks to do good, and he never avoids any opportunity which may present itself for that purpose.

8. The Rosicrucian is not Irritable.

It is evident that a person who works for the benefit of the whole will be hated by those whose personal advantages are not benefited thereby; because selfishness is opposed to magnanimity, and the claims of the few are not always compatible with the interests of the community. The Rosicrucian will therefore be often resisted by narrow-minded and short-sighted people; he will be slandered by caluminators, his motives will be misrepresented, he will be misjudged by the ignorant, ridiculed by the would-be wise, and taunted by the fool. All such proceedings, however, cannot excite or irritate the mind of the true Rosicrucian, nor disturb the divine harmony of his soul; for his faith rests in the perception and knowledge of the truth within himself. The opposition of a thousand ignorant people will not induce him to desist from doing that which he knows to be noble and good, and he will do it even if it should involve the loss of his fortune or of his life. Being able and accustomed to direct his spiritual sight towards the divine, he cannot be deluded by the illusions of matter, but clings to the eternal reality. Being surrounded by angelic influences, and listening to their voices, he is not affected by the noise made by the animals. He lives in the company of those noble beings, who were once men like others, but who have become transfigured, and who are now beyond the reach of the vulgar and low.

9. The Rosicrucian does not think evil of others.

Those who think evil of others see merely the evil which exists within themselves reflected and mirrored forth in others. The Rosicrucian is always willing to recognize in everything that which is good. Tolerance is a virtue by which the Rosicrucian is eminently distinguished from others; and by which he may be known. If a thing appears to be ambiguous, he suspends his judgment about it until he has investigated its nature; but as long as his judgment is not perfect, he is more inclined to form a good opinion than an evil one about everything.

10. The Rosicrucian loves justice.

He, however, never sets himself up as a judge over the faults of others, nor does he wish to appear to be wise by censuring the mistakes of others. He does not enjoy gossip, and cares no more about the foolishness committed by others, than he would about the buzzing of a fly or the capers of a monkey. He finds no pleasure in listening to political or personal quarrels, disputations, or mutual recriminations. He cares nothing for the cunningness of a fox, the dissimulation of a crocodile, or the rapacity of a wolf, and is not amused by the stirring up of mud. His nobility of character lifts him up into a sphere far beyond all such trifles and absurdities, and being above the sensual plane, wherein ordinary mortals find their happiness and enjoyment, he lives with those who do not think evil of each other, who do not rejoice about an injustice done to their brother, or make merry about his ignorance, and enjoy his misfortunes. He enjoys the company of those who love the truth, and who are surrounded by the peace and harmony of the spirit.

11. **The Rosicrucian loves the truth.**

There is no devil worse than falsehood and calumny. Ignorance is a nonentity, but falsehood is the substance of evil. The calumniator rejoices whenever he has found something upon which to base his lies and to make them grow like mountains. Opposed to it is the truth, it being a ray of light from the eternal fountain of GOOD, which has the power to transform man into a divine being. The ROSICRUCIAN seeks, therefore, no other light but the light of truth, and this light he does not enjoy alone, but in company of all who are good and filled with its divine majesty, whether they live on this earth or in the spiritual state; and he enjoys it above all with those who are persecuted, oppressed, and innocent, but who will be saved by the truth.

12. **The Rosicrucian knows how to be silent.**

Those who are false do not love the truth. Those who are foolish do not love wisdom. The true Rosicrucian prefers to enjoy the company of those who can appreciate truth to that of those who would trample it with their feet. He will keep that which he knows locked up within his heart, for in silence is power. As a minister of state does not go about telling to everybody the secrets of the king; so the Rosicrucian does not parade before the public the revelations made to him by the king within, who is nobler and wiser than all the earthly kings and princes; for they only rule by the authority and power derived from Him. His secrecy ceases only when the king commands him to speak, for it is then not he who speaks, but the truth that is speaking through him.

13. **The Rosicrucian believes that which he knows.**

He believes in the immutability of eternal law, and that every cause has a certain effect. He knows that the truth cannot lie, and that the promises made to him by the king will be fulfilled, if he does not himself hinder their fulfilment. He is, therefore, inaccessible to doubt or fear, and puts implicit confidence in the divine principle of truth, which has become alive and conscious within his heart.

14. **The Rosicrucian's hope is firm.**

Spiritual hope is the certain conviction resulting from a knowledge of the law, that the truths recognized by faith will grow and be fulfilled; it is the knowledge of the heart, and very different from the intellectual speculation of the reasoning brain. His faith rests upon the rock of direct perception and cannot be overthrown. He knows that in everything, however evil it may appear to be, there is a germ of good, and he hopes that in the course of evolution that germ will become developed, and thus evil be transformed into good.

15. **The Rosicrucian cannot be vanquished by suffering.**

He knows that there is no light without shadow, no evil without some good, and that strength only grows by resistance. Having once recognized the existence of the Divine principle within everything, external changes are to him of little importance, and do not deserve great attention. His main object is to hold on to his spiritual possessions, and not to lose the crown which he has gained in the battle of life.

16. **The Rosicrucian will always remain a member of his Society.**

Names are of little importance. The principle which presides over the Rosicrucian Society is the truth; and he who knows the truth, and follows it in practice, is a member of the Society over which the truth practises. If all names were changed and all languages altered, the truth would remain the same; and he who lives in the truth will live even if all nations should pass away.

These are the sixteen signs of the true Rosicrucian, which have been revealed to a pilgrim by an angel who took away the heart of the pilgrim, leaving in its place a fiery coal, which is now incessantly burning and glowing with love of the universal brotherhood of humanity.

ROSICRUCIAN JEWELS.

The most valuable jewel of the Rosicrucians is WISDOM, which is represented by a pure DIAMOND in the centre of the ROSE, but the CROSS is adorned with twelve jewels of priceless value, in all of which the power that resides in the truth is manifested. These jewels are:

1. **Jasper** (dark green). The power of active light, multiplying itself to a sevenfold degree, and evolving seven states of the one light, by which the seven states of darkness may be consumed.

2. **Hyacinth** (yellow). LOVE, born from the matrix of light, manifesting itself as it grows, and emitting red rays. Its power overcomes the spirit of anger and violence.

3. **Chrysolite** (white). Princely wisdom. It confounds that which is foolish and vain, subdues it, and comes out of the battle victorious.

4. **Sapphire** (blue). Truth, originating and growing out of its own essence. It overcomes doubt and vacillation.

5. **Smaragd** (green). The blooming spring in its eternal justice, destroying the unjust attributes of a perverted and degenerate nature, and opening the fountain of infinite treasures.

6. **Topaz** (golden). The symbol of peace, mild and pleasant. It suffers no impurity or division to exist, neither does it admit that which causes separation and quarrels. It heals ruptures and cures wounds.

7. **Amethyst** (violet). Impartiality, equilibrium of justice and judgment. It cannot be falsified, bent, or counterfeited. It weighs all things in the scales of justice, and is opposed to fraud, cruelty, or tyranny.

8. **Beryl** (diverse colors). Meekness, humility; the equal temperature of the spirit, being kind and good, and overcoming wrath, stubbornness, and bitterness.

9. **Sardis** (light red). The high magical FAITH, growing into power, and destroying fear, scepticism, and superstition.

10. **Chrysoprase** (light green). Invisible power and strength, overcoming all opposition, allowing nothing to remain which could possibly resist the law.

11. **Sardonyx** (striped). Triumphant JOY and gladness, flowing from the eternal fountain of happiness, destroying all sorrow and sadness.. (May it bless you!).

12. **Chalcedony** (striped). The crown of Victory, dominion, glory. The keystone and the greatest of all miracles, turning everything to the glorification of GOD.

ROSICRUCIAN SYMBOLS

SIGNS FROM THE HEART OF THE CELESTIAL MOTHER.

(From the work of Antonio Ginther. August Vindelicorum. 1741.)

Praenesis. A ship in the open sea, with a floating anchor, and a star shining overhead, with the inscription: *Hac monstrante viam.*

Emblema 1. An open book with the name MARIA, and a heart transfixed by a sword, with the inscription: *Omnibus in omnibus.*

2. A seven-headed monster threatened with a club. Inscription; *In virtute tua.*

3. A closed and sealed door with an angel attempting to open it. Inscription: *Signatur ne perdatur.*

4. A landscape representing an island. The sun rises and the stars shine. Inscription: *Aurora ab lacrymis.*

5. An orange tree bearing fruits, of which the inner part is sweet, while the rind is bitter. Inscription: *Dulce amarum.*

6. An altar with a fire upon it, in which a heart is burning, sending out a sweet odour. Inscription: *In odorem suavitatis.*

7. A pure white lily in a flower-pot, standing in a garden. Inscription: *Virginei laus prima pudoris.*

8. An angel separating wheat from chaff by means of a sieve. Inscription: *Dimittit inanes.*

9. A ring with a jewel exhibited upon a table. Inscription: *Honori invincem.*

10. A globe illuminated by the full moon. Inscription: *Plena sibi et aliis.*

11. Jacob's ladder with seven steps, reaching from the earth up to heaven. Inscription: *Descendendo ascendendo.*

12. A sun-dial attached to the wall of a tower. Inscription: *Altissimus obnumbrat.*

13. The signs of the Zodiac, with the sun passing through the sign of the Virgin. Inscription: *Jam mitius ardet.*

14. A hen brooding in a stable, brooding over eggs. Inscription: *Parit in alieno.*

15. Two palm-trees, inclined towards each other. Inscription: *Blando se pace salutant.*

16. A grape-vine, cut from the trunk, is weeping. Inscription: *Ut gaudeas mero.*

17. A plant, representing a myrrh. Inscription: *Amara sed salubris.*

18. A painter's easel, with a cloth ready for painting. Inscription: *Qua forma placebit.*

19. A heart transfixed by a sword. Inscription: *Usque ad divisionem animae.*

20. Two doves pecking at each other. Inscription: *Amat et castigat.*

21. A passion flower. Inscription: *Delectat et cruciat.*

22. Wolves and sheep, eagles and bats, basking together in the sunshine. Inscription: *Non possentibus offert.*

23. A bird, sitting between thorns and thistles. Inscription: *His ego sustentor.*

24. Ivy winding around a dead tree. Inscription: *Nec mors separavit.*

25. Two hearts in a winepress. Inscription: *Cogit in unum.*

26. A crocodile shedding tears while eating a man. Inscription: *Plorat et devorat.*

27. Wolf devouring a sheep. Inscription: *Non est qui redimat.*

28. Tulips inclining toward the rising sun. Inscription: *Languexit in umbra.*

29. Two stringed musical instruments; a hand plays upon one. Inscription: *Unam tetigis se sat est.*

30. A white lily growing between thorns. Inscription: *Transfixum suavius.*

31. The prophet Jonah thrown into the raging sea. Inscription: *Merger ne mergantur.*

32. The setting sun and the evening star. Inscription: *Sequitur deserta cadentem.*

33. A cross with a snake wound around it. Inscription: *Pharmacumnon venenum.*

34. Eagle, rising towards the sun. Inscription: *Ad te levavi oculos.*

35. A squirrel standing upon a log, floating in the water and rowing. Inscription: *Ne merger.*

36. Light tower, illuminating the ocean. Inscription: *Erantibus una micat.*

37. Rock standing in a stormy sea. Inscription: *Non commovebitur.*

38. A diamond exposed upon a table. Inscription: *In puritate pretium.*

39. Grafting a tree. Inscription: *Accipit in sua.*

40. A man hanging upon a tree. Inscription: *Non est hac tutior umbra.*

41. A flock of sheep, each one bearing the letter T upon the forehead. Inscription: *Non habet redargutionem.*

42. Chandelier with seven lights. Inscription: *Non extinguetur.*

43. A solar eclipse. Inscription: *Morientis sideris umbra.*

44. The setting sun and a rainbow shedding tears. Inscription: *Desinit in lacrymas.*

45. Cypress blown at by winds coming from the four quarters of the world. Inscription: *Concussio firmat.*

46. Two hearts surrounded by thorns, with nails and a dagger. Inscription: *Vulneratum vulnerat.*

47. A heart transfixed by a sword and instruments of torture. Inscription: *Supereminet omnes.*

48. Beehive, and bees flying around flowers. Inscription: *Currit in odorem.*

49. A chemical furnace with retorts, from which drops are falling. Inscription: *Calor elicit imbres.*

50. A man sowing grain into furrows. Inscription: *Ut surgat in ortum.*

51. A cloth spread upon a field and sprinkled with water. Inscription: *A lacrymis candor.*

52. Ocean waves and a bird flying through the furrows of water. Inscription: *Mersa non mergitur.*

53. Noah's dove with an olive branch. Inscription: *Emergere nuntiat orbem.*

54. Flying eagle carrying a lamb. Inscription: *Tulit proedeam tartari.*

55. Rain descending upon flowers. Inscription: *Dulce refrigerium.*

56. Plumb-line and level. Inscription: *Recta a recto.*

57. A hot iron upon an anvil. Inscription: *Dum calet.*

58. Solitary bird sitting in a cave. Inscription: *Gemit dilectum suum.*

59. Elephant drinking blood, flowing from a grape. Inscription: *Acuitur in praelium.*

60. Bird escaping from a nest. Inscription: *Ad sidera sursum.*

61. Sunrise rays shining into a heart of adamant. Inscription: *Intima lustrat.*

62. A flying bird attached to a string. Inscription: *Cupio dissolvi.*

63. Two birds of Paradise flying upwards. Inscription: *Innixa ascendit.*

64. A triple crown made of silver, iron, and gold. Inscription: *Curso completo.*

65. The statue of Dagon thrown down and broken to pieces. A corpse. Inscription: *Cui honorem honorem.*

66. The Red Sea dividing for the passage of the Israelites. Inscription: *Illue iter quo ostendum.*

67. Labyrinth with a human figure therein. A hand extended from heaven holds a thread reaching down to the figure. Inscription: *Hac duce tuta via est.*

68. A camp. Among the tents is a standard bearing the image of a man. Inscription: *Praesidium et decus.*

69. A clock, whose finger points to the second hour. Inscription: *Ultima secunda.*

70. Ship at sea carrying a light. Fishes and birds are attracted by the glow. Inscription: *Veniunt ad lucem.*

Epilogus.—Noah's ark in tranquil water. Inscription: *Non mergitur, sed extollitur.*

SIGNS REFERRING TO THE DIVINE CHILD.

Praenesis.—A hen with chickens under her wings. A hawk preying in the air above. Inscription: *Sub umbra alarum tuarum.*

Emblema 1. A figure kneeling and holding a book wherein is represented a fiery heart. Inscription: *Tolle lege.*

2. Altar upon which a fire is lighted by a sunray. Inscription: *Extinctos suscitat ignes.*

3. Sunray falling through a lens and setting a ship on fire. Inscription: *Ignis ab Primo.*

4. Sun shining upon a lambskin extended upon the earth. Inscription: *Descendit de coe is.*

5. A chrysalis upon a leaf. Inscription: *Ecce venio.*

7. The sea and the rising sun. Inscription: *Renovabit faciem terrae.*

8. A rising sun eclipsed by the moon. Inscription: *Condor ut exorior.*

9. A chicken and an eagle in the air. The former is protected against the latter by a shield. Inscription: *A facie persequentis.*

10. A rose in the midst of a garden. Inscription: *Haec mihi sola placet.*

11. A lamb burning upon an altar. Inscription: *Deus non despicies.*

12. Dogs hunting. Inscription: *Fuga salutem.*

13. A lamb dying at the foot of a cross. Inscription: *Obediens usque ad mortem.*

14. The ark of the covenant. Rays of lightning. Inscription: *Procul este profani.*

15. Sun in the midst of clouds. Inscription: *Fulgura in pluvium fuit.*

16. Sun shining upon sheep and wolves. Inscription: *Super robos et malos.*

17. A well and a pitcher. Inscription: *Hauriar, non exhauriar.*

18. Animals entering the ark. Inscription: *Una salutem.*

19. Shepherd carrying a lamb. Inscription: *Onus meum leve.*

20. Sheep drinking at a well. The water is stirred by a pole. Inscription: *Similem dant vulnera formam.*

21. A dove sitting upon a globe. Inscription: *Non sufficit una.*

22. Light penetrating the clouds. Inscription: *Umbram fugat veritas.*

23. A vineyard and the rising sun. Inscription: *Pertransiit beneficiendo.*

24. Three hearts with a sieve floating above them. Inscription: *Cœlo contrito resurgent.*

25. Swan cleaning his feathers before proceeding to eat. Inscription: *Antequam comedum.*

26. A hungry dog howling at the moon. Inscription: *Inanis impetus.*

27. Ark of the covenant drawn by two oxen. Inscription: *Sancta sancte.*

28. A winepress. Inscription: *Premitur ut exprimat.*

29. An opening bud. Inscription: *Vulneribus profundit opes.*

30. Amor shooting arrows at a heart. Inscription: *Donec attingam.*

31. Cross and paraphernalia for crucification. Inscription: *Praebet non prohibet.*

32. A sunflower looking towards the rising sun. Inscription: *Usque ad occasum.*

33. Drops of sweat falling down in a garden. Inscription: *Tandem resoluta venit.*

34. Sword protruding from the clouds. Inscription: *Caedo noncedo.*

35. Hammer and anvil, a forge and a fire. Inscription: *Ferendo, non feriendo.*

36. A ram crowned with thorns upon an altar. Inscription: *Victima coronata.*

37. A sheep carrying animals. Inscription: *Quam grave portat onus.*

38. A crucified person and a snake upon a tree. Inscription: *Unde mors unde vita.*

39. A tree shedding tears into three dishes. Inscription: *Et laesa medelam.*

40. A spring fountain. Inscription: *Rigat ut erigat.*

41. A heart offered to an eagle. Inscription: *Redibit ad Dominum.*

42. A heart upon a cross surrounded by thorns, crowned with a laurel. Inscription: *Pignus amabile pacis.*

43. Bird persecuted by a hawk seeks refuge in the cleft of a rock. Inscription: *Hoc tuta sua sub antro.*

44. Target with a burning heart in the centre; Amor shooting arrows at it. Inscription: *Trahe mi post te.*

45. Pelican feeding her young ones with her own blood. Inscription: *Ut vitam habeant.*

47. Phœnix sinking into the flames. Inscription: *Hic mihi dulce mori.*

48. Blood from a lamb flowing into a cup. Inscription: *Purgantes temperat ignis.*

49. Clouds from which proceed rays of lightning. Inscription: *Lux recto fatumque noscenti.*

50. Eagle flying towards the sun. Inscription: *Tunc facie ad faciem.*

Epilogus.—A hedgehog, having rolled in fruits, is covered with them. Inscription: *Venturi providus aevi.*

He who can see the meaning of all these allegories has his eyes open.

Every Postulant in the Congregation of the Outer is expected to make these principles, practices, and tenets of the Fraternity a part of his or her daily life, thought and action.

They are not mere generalities. One who looks for sensation, miracle or phenomena will undoubtedly be disappointed, and to such they will be of no effect. We safely assert, however, that the Ego that is so far advanced as to be beyond the study, practice and application of these concepts, has so far advanced along the spiritual pathway as to have no need for the ministration of this Fraternity.

It will be found that the personal application of these conceptions will require will power, strength of mind, and persistence, and they are the fundamental requirements of progress in spiritual attainment and development.

By making these principles and doctrines a part of one's daily life, they will enable such an one to reply definitely, positively and accurately on all questions properly and legitimately asked, concerning the attitude of the Fraternity regarding the vital problems of humanity.

The Fraternity now publishes a "Standard Text Book," entitled "Rosicrucian Fundamentals." The book is a digest of the Rosicrucian synthesis of Religion, Science and Philosophy. This book is the one recommended and used in our colleges by beginners in the Art. Thereafter each student is taught how to seek and attain knowledge from higher sources than books, which, after all, are but the expressions of their authors' conceptions on a given subject. The Fraternity, however, is not a publisher. Some of its lessons, lectures, etc., are printed and bound up for easy distribution, but they must be purchased directly from the publishing company whose name and address has already been given. The Society makes no profit on any of them.

As a Postulant, you are at liberty to invite to membership any man or woman of good character, from the ages of sixteen in the case of ladies and from twenty-one in the case of gentlemen. Dues in local colleges are such as each college may provide for in its own by-laws. Fees for members in the Congregation of the Outer, until such time as this class of members become affiliated with a local college, are $8.50 affiliation fee, and $3.50 dues per annum.

Annual dues in the Congregation of the Outer are payable January second of each year. The High Council has no paid officers. All moneys received by the Society go direct to the work of its propaganda, and the Society at all times is grateful for such contributions, donations and bequests as its members feel disposed to make. No individual member profits either directly or indirectly in a pecuniary manner.

It is expected, and earnestly hoped, that **You**, as a member of the Congregation of the Outer, to whom this brochure comes, may so imbibe the spirit of true Rosicrucianism that you will become a power in our work and **Art.**

Each member of the Congregation of the Outer should make it his or her highest ambition to interest sufficient friends in the work to ensure the institution and chartering of a regular College in such member's home city or town. All possible assistance, instruction, and co-operation will be given from the High Council. It is our intent to make Rosicrucianism a powerful factor in the work and activity of humanity thruout these United States. We trust **You** can be relied upon as one of our most active co-operators.

In the section devoted to stating the Society's attitude toward the subject of **Rest** you were informed that a practice of concentration would be given you later in the work.

Briefly, it is this. From the time you commence active work with us, make this part of your daily regime. On retiring, before committing yourself to the contemplation of oblivion, go over in retrospect the events of the day. Begin always with the events just before retiring and work back toward the beginning of the day. The reason for this will be given you later. As you consider each event, weigh it carefully, judge yourself, your attitude, at the time the event occurred and at the time you are concentrating upon it. Decide as to the right or wrong of your own position, and if you find yourself to have been wrong, make it your imperative first duty on the following day, to rectify that wrong attitude so far as in your power lies. By so doing you will in large measure assimilate the experience it is the purpose of your present incarnation to acquire, and further, you will prevent the accumulation of Karma which otherwise might require another incarnation to discharge. Then, bring visually before your spiritual contemplation the symbol of the Cross and Rose of the Order, and ascertain what message it may have for **You** personally. It is a good idea to send us such impressions as you may receive, and see how far they approach to the true symbolism they are designed to express.

With the truest and most cordial sentiments of brotherhood and fraternalism, we welcome you to your present stage of membership, and anticipate your further progress amongst us.

"Rosicrucian Orders."

Reprinted from "In the Pronaos of the Temple".

By Dr. Franz Hartmann, 1890.

WHY is there so much perplexity about the mysterious order of the Rosicrucians? Let us ask in return, Why is there so much perplexity about that mysterious being called "Man"? The answer is that man is a spiritual being, inhabiting the spiritual world, which he has never entirely left; while the terrestrial personality in which he manifests himself during his earthly life is an inhabitant of this planet. That which the historian and the scientist know about man is merely that which refers to his physical body; while nothing is known to them about his real self. To imagine that such knowledge is true anthropology is like imagining that we know all about a man if we once see the coat which he wears. Likewise the true Rosicrucians, whether they still walk upon the earth in a visible form, or whether they inhabit the astral plane, are spiritual powers, such as are beyond the reach of examination of the externally reasoning historian or scientist. They are people who, as the Bible expresses it, "live upon the earth, but whose consciousness is in heaven."

The vulgar sees only the external form, but not the spirit which is the true inhabitant of that form. To discern the latter, the power of spiritual discernment is required. The coat which a man wears does not make the man; to pour water over a person does not make him a true Christian, and to have one's name entered into the register of some society calling itself "Rosicrucian," does not endow one with the rosy and golden light of love and wisdom that comes from the unfoldment of the "Rose" within the centre of one's soul.

But it is far easier to undergo some external ceremony than to die the mystic death which is required for the purpose of passing through the "Gates of Gold"; it is easier to profess a creed than to acquire true knowledge; and for this reason we find during the Middle Ages not less than at this present time many people who imagine that they could be made into Rosicrucians and Adepts, by joining some society dealing with mystical subjects.

In the beginning of the 17th century Germany was overrun, not only by monks and nuns and religious fanatics of all kinds, but also by a great many impostors and adventurers. There were pretended Alchemists, Astrologers, Fortune-tellers, and there was a universal mania among the people to pry into the secrets of Nature, and to enrich themselves by alchemical processes, or, if need be, by the help of the devil. This epidemic of superstition and folly seemed to require a strong remedy, and as foolish people are not accessible to reasonable arguments, it occurred to some sharp-witted mind to try the more caustic remedy of sarcasm. There appeared in the year 1614 two pamphlets, written by the same author, entitled, *"Universal and General Reformation of the Whole Wide World,"* and the *"Fama Fraternitatis; or, Brotherhood of the Laudable Order of R.C.* (Rosicrucians), *a message to the Governments, nobles, and scientists of Europe."* This book was out of print during the last century, and Frederic Nicolai, in Berlin, had it reprinted in the year 1781, falsifying, however, its date, inserting 1681 instead of the correct date, and "Regenburg" instead of "Berlin." Another edition of the *Fama Fraternitatis* appeared at Frankfort-on-Maine in the year 1827, and to this was added an additional part, entitled *"Confessio."*

These books, soon after they first appeared, made a great impression upon the public mind, and were immediately translated into several languages. The

Universal Reformation is a satirical work. Its most interesting contents are an account of the meeting of a supposed Congress for the purpose of reforming the world. The story is as follows:—At the time of the Emperor Justinian, *Apollo* takes a look at the world, and finds it to be full of vices and wickedness. He therefore makes up his mind to call together a meeting of all the wise and virtuous men of the country to consult together how this evil might be remedied. Unfortunately, among all of them there is none to be found who is possessed of sufficient virtue and intelligence to give the desired advice. Apollo therefore assembles the seven ancient sages of Greece and three Romans, *Marcus*, *Cato*, and *Seneca*. A young Italian philosopher, by the name of *Jacob Mazzonius*, is appointed secretary. The congregation meets in the delphic Palatium; and now follow the speeches which were held. The sages talk the most egregious nonsense. *Thales*, for instance, advises that a window should be inserted in the breast of every man, so that the people could look into his heart. *Solon* has become a communist, and wants to divide out all the public and private property, so that all should have equal parts. *Bias* proposes to prohibit all intercourse between the people, to destroy the bridges and to forbid using ships. *Cato* desires that God should be asked to send another deluge, to destroy the whole feminine sex and all males over 20 years of age; and to request Him to invent a new and better method of procreation. All the sages dispute and contradict each other, and finally it is resolved to cite the diseased century and make it come into court, so that the patient may be closely investigated. The century is brought in. It is an old man with a healthy-looking face, but having a weak voice. They examine him, and find that his face is painted, and a further investigation shows that not a single part of his body is without some disease. The savants then come to the conclusion that they cannot cure him; but they do not want to adjourn without having it appear that they had done something very useful and important, so they impose a new tax upon cabbage, carrots and parsley. They publish the document with a great deal of swagger and self-praise, and the delighted people jubilate and applaud.

The meaning of this pamphlet, which was written for the purpose of throwing ridicule upon a certain class of people who wanted to improve the world at once and to show the absurdity and impossibility of such an undertaking, was plain enough, and it seems incredible that its purpose should have been misunderstood. That there were any people who took the matter seriously shows the extreme ignorance and want of judgment of the common people of those times, and forms an interesting episode for the student of history and intellectual evolution. The other pamphlet which accompanied the former is the celebrated *Fama Fraternitatis*. The *Universal Reformation* threw ridicule upon the self-constituted "world-reformers," and this second pamphlet now invites these would-be reformers to meet, and it, at the same time, gives them some useful hints as to what they might do to attain their object; advising them that the only true method for improving the world is to begin by improving themselves. This pamphlet being like the other one, a satire upon the would-be reformers and so-called Rosicrucians, might, for all that, have been written by a genuine Rosicrucian, for it contains true Rosicrucian principles, such as are advocated by the Adepts. It shows the insufficiency of the scientific and theological views of those times. It ridicules the imbecility of the *pretended* Alchemists, who imagined that by some *chemical* process they could transform lead into gold; but in doing so it gives good advice, and under the mask of divulging the laws and objects of some mysterious Rosicrucian Society, it indicates certain rules and principles, which afterward formed the basis of an organized society of investigators in Occultism, who adopted the name *Rosicrucians*.

Added to this, *Fama Fraternitatis* is the story of the "pious, spiritual, and highly-illuminated Father," Fr. R. C., *Christian Rosencreutz*. It is said that he was a German nobleman, who had been educated in a convent, and that long before the time of the Reformation he had made a pilgrimage to the Holy Land in company with another brother of this convent, and that while at Damascus they had been initiated by some learned Arabs into the mysteries of the secret science. After remaining three years at Damascus, they went to Fez, in Africa, and there they obtained still more knowledge of magic, and of the relations existing between the macrocosm and microcosm. After having also travelled in Spain, he returned to Germany, where he founded a kind of a convent called *Sanctus Spiritus*, and remained there writing his secret science and continuing his studies. He then accepted as his assistants, at first three, and afterwards four more monks from the same convent in which he had been educated, and thus founded the first society of the Rosicrucians. They then laid down the results of their science in books, which are said to be still in existence, and in the hands of some Rosicrucians. It is then said that 120 years after his death, the entrance to his tomb was discovered. A staircase led into a subterranean vault, at the door of which was written, *Post annos CXX. patebo.* There was a light burning in the vault, which however, became extinct as soon as it was approached. The vault had seven sides and seven angles, each side being five feet wide and eight feet high. The upper part represented the firmament, the floor the earth, and they were laid out in triangles, while each side was divided into ten squares. In the middle was an altar, bearing a brass plate, upon which were engraved the letters, *A. C. R. C.*, and the words *Hoc Universi Compendium vivus mihi Sepulchrum feci.* In the midst were four figures surrounded by the words, *Nequaquam Vacuum. Legis Jugum. Libertas Evangelii. Dei Gloria Intacta.* Below the altar was found the body of *Rosencreuz*, intact, and without any signs of putrefaction. In his hand was a book of parchment, with golden letters marked on the cover with a T (Testamentum?), and at the end was written, *Ex Deo nascimur. In Jesu morimur. Per Spiritum Sanctum reviviscimus."* There were signed the names of the brothers present at the funeral of the deceased.

In the year 1615, a new edition of these pamphlets appeared, to which was added another one, entitled *Confessio;* or, "the Confession of the Society and Brotherhood of the R. C.;" giving great promises about future revelations, but ending with the advice to everybody that until these revelations were made the people should continue to believe in the Bible.

All these pamphlets had—as will be shown farther on—one and the same author, and as the *"General Reformation"* was of an entirely satirical character and a pure invention, having no more foundation, in fact, than the *Don Quixote de la Mancha* of *Cervantes*, there is no reason whatever why we should believe that the succeeding pamphlets should have been meant seriously, and that the story of the returned knight, *Christian Rosencreuz*, should have been anything more than an allegory. Moreover, there is no indication of what became of the body of that knight after it was once discovered, nor that the temple of the Holy Ghost (Sanctus Spiritus) exists anywhere else but in the hearts of men.

The whole object of these pamphlets seems to have been to present great truths to the ignorant, but to dish them up in a fictitious form, appealing to the curiosity of the people, and to the prevailing craving for a knowledge of the mysteries of Nature, which the majority of the people of these times wanted to know for the purpose of obtaining selfish and personal benefits.

The beauty of the doctrines which shone through these satirical writings were so great and attractive that they excited universal attention; but at the same time the craving of the majority of the people for the mysterious was so great that it blinded their eyes ,and rendered them incapable of perceiving the true object of the writer, which was to ridicule the pretensions of dogmatic science and theology, and to draw the people up to a higher conception of true Christianity. The belief in the existence of a real secret organization of Rosicrucians, possessed of the secret how to make gold out of lead and iron, and of prolonging life by means of taking some fluid in the shape of a medicine, was universal; and quacks and pretenders of all kinds roamed over the country and helped to spread the superstitions, often selling worthless compounds for fabulous prices as being the "Elixir of Life;" while others wasted their fortunes and became poor in making vain efforts to transmute metals.

A flood of writings appeared, some attacking and some defending the Rosicrucian Society, which was supposed to exist, but of which no one knew anything. Some people, and even some of the well-informed ones, believed in the existence of such a society; others denied it. But neither one class nor the other could bring any positive proofs for their beliefs. People are always willing to believe that which they desire to be true, and everyone wanted to be admitted as a member of that secret society, of which nobody was certain whether it existed at all; and if anyone boasted of being a Rosicrucian, or succeeded in creating the impression that he was one, he awed the ignorant, and was regarded by them as a very favoured person, and in this way impostors and adventurers often succeeded in preying upon the pockets of the rich.

Those who wanted to be taught magic and sorcery desired that a society or school where they might learn such things should exist; and because they desired it they believed in its existence. If no genuine Rosicrucian could be found, one had to be invented. If the true Rosicrucian society was not to be had, imitations of what was believed to constitute a Rosicrucian society had to be organized. In this way numerous societies were formed, calling themselves "Rosicrucians"; and "Rosicrucianism" took various shapes.

One of the most important publications, and which is calculated to throw light upon the mysterious subject of Rosicrucianism which still perplexes the learned, is the *Chymical Marriage of Christian Rosencreutz*, printed in 1616. This, again, was written to throw ridicule upon the vain and self-conceited dogmatists, scientists, and "gold-makers" of those times, while at the same time it contains high and exalted truths, disguised in an allegorical form, but easily to be perceived by the practical Occultist, *and by him only*. It can easily be seen that the style and tendencies of this publication have a great deal of resemblance to that of the *Fama Fraternitatis*. Now it has been ascertained beyond any doubt that the author of the "Chemical Marriage" was Johann Valentine Andreae,* who wrote it while a young student in the years 1602 and 1603 in Tübingen. He acknowledges this in the history which he gives of his life, and he adds that he intended to give a true picture of the popular follies of that time. This renders it extremely probable that he was also the author of the "General Reformation," of the *Confessio*, and of the story of Christian Rosencreutz, and this probability amounts to almost conviction if we take into consideration the discovery made afterwards, that the "General Reformation" is nothing else but a literal translation of a part of a book from Boccalini's *Ragguagli di Parnasso*. Andreae was a great admirer of that author, and he also adopted his style in his *Mythologia Christiana*; it is therefore plain that he also made the above-named translation, and added it to his "Fama Fraternitatis." Both writings, in fact, form a complement to each other. In the "General Reformation" the political would-be reformers are held up to ridicule, and in the "Fama" the mystical dreamers, imaginary theosophists, pretended gold-makers, and supposed discoverers of the universal panacea are castigated. There can be no reasonable doubt that this was Andreae's object, and, moreover, his intimate friend, Professor Besoldt, in Tübingen, acknowledged it in saying that the character of both books was plain enough, and that it was very strange that so many intelligent people had been led by the nose to mistake their meaning. Andreae himself, without, however, acknowledging himself to be their author, expressed himself to the effect that the whole was a satire and a fable. In his "confession" he says: (Sc.) *risisse semper Rosicrucianam fabulum et curiositatis fraterculos fuisse in sectatum*† and in his paper entitled "*Turris Babel, seu judiciorum de Fraternitatae Rosaccae crucis chaos*," he speaks still more plainly upon this subject. It seems to have been his object in this latter publication to help those to become sober again who had become intoxicated by misunderstanding the former publications, for he exclaims: "Listen, ye mortals! In vain will ye wait for the arrival of

---

Dr. Johann Valentin Andreae was born Aug. 17, 1586, at Herrenberg, in Wurtemberg, and died an abbot of Adelsberg, at Stuttgart, June 27, 1654. He spoke several languages, was well versed in theology, mathematics, history, and the natural sciences. He was of a noble mind, anxious to do good, and an original character. Herder describes him as a rose among the thorns.

† Andreae's autobiography. *Weismann*, hist. eccl. P. ii., p. 936.

that fraternity; the comedy is over. The *fama* has played it in, the *fama* has played it out," etc., etc. Still there were many who were not satisfied with this explanation, and who believed that it had been Andreae's intention to cause by his *fama*, a secret society of the scientists of his age to come into existence; but Andreae was too wise to attempt such an absurdity and to apply to the most *unreasonable* persons of his age to form a *reasonable* society.

The question why he should have selected the name "Rosicrucian" for his imaginary society is not difficult to answer. The *Cross* and the *Rose* were favourite symbols among the Alchemists and Theosophists long before anything of a "Rosicrucian Society" was known. Moreover, in his own coat of arms, as in that of Luther, there was a cross and four roses, a circumstance which probably led him to select that name.

There is, perhaps, very rarely a fable or work of fiction invented which is not based upon some fact, however disconnected such facts may be with the subject. A work, entitled *Sphinx Rosacea*, printed in 1618, makes it appear very plausible that the writer of the *Fama Fraternitatis*, in inventing the story of *Christian Rosencreutz* and his three brothers, whose number was afterwards increased by four more, had certain originals in his mind, which served as proto-types to construct his story. The author of that *Sphinx* says that the idea of forming such a society for the general reformation of mankind arose from the success of Luther's Reformation; that the knight, Christian Rosencreutz, was, in reality, no other person than a certain *Andreas von Carolstadt*, an adventurer, who had travelled a great deal, but never been in Palestine. He made himself so obnoxious to the clergy of his time, whom he desired to reform, that they, after his death, put the following *Epitaph* upon his grave:—*Carolstadius Pestis Ecclesiae venonissima, tandem a Diabolo occisus est.* This means: "Here lies Carolstadt, who was a poisonous plague to the Church until the devil killed him at last." The three supposed associates of Rosencreutz were the friends of Carolstadt, the reformer *Zwingi, Oecolompadius*, and *Bucerus*, and the four others, who were supposed to have been added afterwards, were probably *Nicalaus Palargus, Marcus Stubner, Martin Cellurius*, and, finally *Thomas Münster*, all of which persons were more or less known on account of their desire to aid in reforming the Church.

As the people became infatuated with the idea of becoming Rosicrucians, and no real society of Adepts could be found, they organized Rosicrucian societies without any real Adepts, and thus a great many so-called Rosicrucian societies came into existence. There was one such society founded by *Christian Rose* in 1622, having head centres in the Hague, Amsterdam, Nuremberg, Mantua, Venice, Hamburg, Dantzig and Erfurt. They used to dress in black, and wore at their meetings blue ribbons with a golden wreath and a rose. As a sign of recognition the brothers wore a black silk cord in the top button hole. This ornament was given to the neophytes after they had promised under oath to be strangled by such a cord rather than reveal the secrets which they were supposed to possess. They also had another sign, consisting of the "tonsure," such as is used today by the Roman Catholic clergy, meaning a small round shaven spot on the top of the head, originating probably from the custom of the Buddhist priests, who shave their whole head. Hence many of them wore a wig, in order not to be recognized as belonging to the brotherhood. They led a very quiet life, and were devout people. On all high festivals, very early at sunrise they would leave their residence, and go out through the gate of the town facing the east. When another one of them appeared, cr when they met at other places, one would say: *Ave Frater!* to which the other would answer, *Rosae et Aureae;* then the first one said *Crucis*, then both together said: *Benedictus Deus Dominus noster, qui nobis dedit Signum!* They also had for the sake of legitimation a large document, to which the *Imperator* affixed the great seal.*

There was another "Rosicrucian society," formed at Paris in the year 1660 by an apothecary named *Jacob Rose*. This society was dissolved in 1674, in consequence of the notorious case of wholesale poisoning by the ill-reputed Marquise de Brinvillier.

* Extracted from the "Sphinx." Vol. I., No. 1.

Whether or not there ever were any real Adepts and genuine Alchemists among the members of these Rosicrucian societies, we are, of course, not in a position to affirm. We are satisfied to know that Adepts do exist and that Alchemy is a fact; but whether they had anything to do with these orders we do not know, nor do we care about it, as it is now of no consequence whatever. All that we know for certain in regard to this matter is, that there existed at that time persons in possession of an extraordinary amount of occult knowledge, as is shown by the books they have left; but whether these persons belonged or did not belong to any organized society, is absolutely useless to know.

During the life of *Theophrastus Paracelsus*, he was the intellectual centre to which Alchemists, Occultists, Mystics, Reformers and Rosicrucians were attracted, but there is no indication that he was a member of any society of men calling themselves "Rosicrucians." There is, likewise, no indication that after the time of Paracelsus any organized society of true Adepts, calling themselves "Rosicrucian Society," ever existed. Some of the greatest minds of that age were engaged in occult research, and were naturally attracted together by the bonds of sympathy; but however much they may have been united in the spirit (in the temple of the Holy Ghost), there is no indication that they had an organized society on the external plane, nor would any *real* Adepts need any other but spiritual signs of recognition.

A book printed in 1714, and written by *Sincerus Renatus*, contains the remarkable information that some years ago the *Masters* of the Rosicrucians had gone to India, and that none of them at present remained in Europe. This is not at all improbable; for the moral atmosphere of Europe is at the present time not very congenial for spiritual development, nor very inviting to those who, while progressing on the Path of Light, are reincarnating in physical forms.

As all researches after a real Rosicrucian society consisting of genuine Adepts were naturally fruitless, the excitement caused by the *Fama fraternitatis* gradually ceased, and there was not much said or written about them until between the years 1756 and 1768, when a new degree of Freemasonry came into existence, called the "Rosicrucian Knights, or the order of *Rose-croix*, or the *Knights of the Eagle and Pelican;* but we should in vain search among these knights for any genuine Adept, or even for anyone possessed of occult knowledge or power; for as our modern churches have lost the key to the mysteries which were once entrusted to their guardianship, and have degenerated into places for social gatherings and religious pastime, so our modern Masons have long ago lost the *Word*, and will not find it again unless they dive below the surface of external ceremonies and seek for it in their own hearts.

The most important books written during the time of the Rosicrucian controversy were the following:—

I. Books Written in Favour of the Rosicrucians:—

(Titles translated from the German.)

Fama Fraternitatis, or the discovery of the laudable Order of the Rosy Cross.—*Anonym*, Frankfurt, 1615.

Confessio, or Confession of the Fraternity of the Rosy Cross.—*Anonym.*, Frankfurt, 1615.

Opinion regarding the laudable Order of the Rosy Cross, by *Adam Bruxius*, M. D., 1616.

Message to the Philosophical Fraternity of the Rosy Cross, by *Valentin Tschirnessus*, Goerlitz.

Thesaurus Fidei, or warning to the novices of the Fraternity of the Rosy Cross, 1619.

Fons Gratiae, by *Trenaeus Agnostus*, C. W. 1619.

Raptus Philosophicus, or Philosophical Revelations for the Fraternity of the R. C., 1619, by *Rhodophilus Stansophorus*.

Silentium Post Clamores. An apology resp. Defence, by *R.M.F.*. 1617.

Frater Crucis Rosacae, or, What kind of people are the Rosicrucians? By *M.A.O.F.W.*, 1617.

Speculum Constantiae. Appeal to new members of the R. C. Society, by *Irenaeus Agnostus, C.W.*, 1618.

Themis Aurea.. The Laws and Regulations of the laudable Fraternity of the R.C., by *Michael Maier, Imp. Cons. Com. Eq. Ex.*, 1618.

Tintinabulum Sapnorum, or, The Discovery of the blessed Fraternity of the Order of the R.C., by *Irenaeus Agnostus, C.W.*, 1619.

Frater Non Frater. Admonitions to the disciples of the R.C., 1619.

Prodromus Rhodo-Stauroticus. Directions for the practice of Alchemy, 1620.

Colloquium Rhodo-Stauroticum. A discourse regarding the Fraternity of the R.C., 1621.

Rosencreutz Ch. Chemical Marriage, Anno 1459? (1781).

II. Writings Inimical to the Rosicrucians.

Benevolent Advice regarding the Fama and Confessio of the R.C., by *And. Libarius M.D., P.C., Sac. Theolog. and Philosoph.*, 1616.

Sphinx, Rosacea. Suspicions in regard to the mysteries of the R.C., by *Christophorus Nigrinus Philomusus and Theologus*, 1618.

The New Arabian and Moorish Fraternity, by *Eusebius Christianus,* a carrier of the wooden cross.

Speculum Ambitionis, or *A Mirror for Ambition,* in which may be seen how the Devil has brought all sorts of new orders into existence. A refutation of the doctrines of that new sect, called Rosicrucians, by *Joh. Hintner,* 1620.

Tomfoolery Discovered, or, Christian Refutation of the so-called Brothers of the Rosy Cross, showing that these people are not of God, but the Devil. A timely warning to all pious Christians. By *Joh. Silvert Aegl,* 1617.

The more important modern books on Rosicrucianism are: *Semler's* "Collections to the history of the Rosicrucians"; *Bouterwek's* "Origin of the R.C.; *Murr,* "The true origin of Rosicrucians and Freemasons"; *Buhle,* "Origin and history of the R C."; *Nicolai,* "Remarks about the history of the Rosicrucians and Freemasons"; *Herder,* "An article in the German *Mercury* of March, 1782, and reprinted in Herder's *Philosophy and History,*" vol. 15, p. 258; *Arnold,* "History of the churches and heretics," part ii., lib. xvii., cap. 18; *Rossbach,* "Joh. Valentin Andreae and his age," Berlin, 1819. There are numerous books on Alchemy, Theosophy, and Occult Science which have been written by people supposed to have been Rosicrucians; but they give no account of the history of the latter. The most prominent are the works of *Theophrastus Paracelsus, Jacob Boehme, Cornelius Agrippa of Nettesheim; Robert Fludd's* "Summum Bonum"; *John Arndt,* "Silentium Dei," and "The true Christendom"; *Simon Studion,* "Naometria"; *Trenaeus Philalethes,* "Lumen de Lumina," and innumerable others, which may be drawn into this category; but perhaps the most interesting of all is an illustrated work which is now out of print, and has become very rare, and which is entitled "*The Secret Symbols of the Rosicrucians of the Sixteenth and Seventeenth Century,*" and from which a great deal of information contained in this present volume is taken.

The Rosicrucian Classics.

The Fama Fraternitatis
The Confessio of the Rosicrucian Fraternity
The Chymical Marriage of Christian Rosencreutz

Reprinted from "The Real History of the Rosicrucians"
By Arthur Edward Waite, 1887.

Editor's note:—Mr. Arthur Edward Waite is one of the most painstaking apologists and writers on the subjects of Rosicrucian and Masonic history, and his works have the enviable merit of all possible accuracy. His valuable work referred to above is long since out of print, and we therefore offer the following reprint of portions of it, in order that all our fraters may have the benefit of a good text of otherwise unobtainable translations and renditions of these three famous Rosicrucian treatises, around which so much controversy and speculation have been built.

The Fama Fraternitatis.

THE FAMA FRATERNITATIS OF THE MERITORIOUS ORDER OF THE ROSY CROSS, ADDRESSED TO THE LEARNED IN GENERAL, AND THE GOVERNORS OF EUROPE.

The original edition of the "Universal Reformation" contained the manifesto bearing the above title, but which the notary Haselmeyer declares to have existed in manuscript as early as the year 1610, as would also appear from a passage in the Cassel edition of 1614, the earliest which I have been able to trace. It was reprinted with the "Confessio Fraternitatis" and the "Allgemeine Reformation der Ganzen Welt" at Franckfurt-on-the-Mayne in 1615. A Dutch translation was also published in this year, and by 1617 there had been four Franckfurt editions, the last omitting the "Universal Reformation," which, though it received an elaborate alchemical elucidation by Brotoffer,[1] seems gradually to have dropped out of notice. "Other editions," says Buhle, "followed in the years immediately succeeding, but these it is unnecessary to notice. In the title-page of the third Franckfurt edition stands—*First printed at Cassel* in the year 1616. But the four first words apply to the original edition, the four last to this.[2]

Fama Fraternitatis; or, a Discovery of the Fraternity of the Most Laudable Order of the Rosy Cross.

Seeing the only wise and merciful God in these latter days hath poured out so richly His mercy and goodness to mankind, whereby we do attain more and more to the perfect knowledge of His Son Jesus Christ and of Nature, that justly we may boast of the happy time wherein there is not only discovered unto us the half part of the world, which was heretofore unknown and hidden, but He hath also made manifest unto us many wonderful and never-heretofore seen

---

[1] "Elucidarius Major, oder Erleuchterunge über die Reformation der ganzen Weiten Welt . . . Durch Radtichs Brotofferr." 1617.

[2] De Quincey, "Rosicrucians and Freemasons."

works and creatures of Nature, and, moreover, hath raised men, indued with great wisdom, which might partly renew and reduce all arts (in this our spotted and imperfect age) to perfection, so that finally man might thereby understand his own nobleness and worth, and why he is called *Microcosmus*, and how far his knowledge extendeth in Nature.

Although the rude world herewith will be but little pleased, but rather smile and scoff thereat ; also the pride and covetousness of the learned is so great, it will not suffer them to agree together ; but were they united, they might, out of all those things which in this our age God doth so richly bestow on us, collect *Librum Naturae*, or, a Perfect Method of all Arts. But such is their opposition that they still keep, and are loath to leave, the old course, esteeming Porphyry, Aristotle, and Galen, yea, and that which hath but a meer show of learning, more than the clear and manifested Light and Truth. Those, if they were now living, with much joy would leave their erroneous doctrines ; but, here is too great weakness for such a great work. And although in Theologie, Physic, and the Mathematic, the truth doth oppose it itself, nevertheless, the old Enemy, by his subtilty and craft, doth show himself in hindering every good purpose by his instruments and contentions wavering people.

To such an intention of a general reformation, the most godly and highly-illuminated Father, our Brother, C. R. C., a German, the chief and original of our Fraternity, hath much and long time laboured, who, by reason of his poverty (although descended of noble parents), in the fifth year of his age was placed in a cloyster, where he had learned indifferently the Greek and Latin tongues, and (upon his earnest desire and request), being yet in his growing years, was associated to a Brother, P. A. L., who had determined to go to the Holy Land. Although this Brother dyed in Ciprus, and so never came to Jerusalem, yet our Brother C. R. C. did not return, but shipped himself over, and went to Damasco, minding from thence to go to Jerusalem. But by reason of the feebleness of his body he remained still there, and by his skill in physic he obtained much favour with the Turks, and in the meantime he became acquainted with the Wise Men of Damcar in Arabia, and beheld what great wonders they wrought, and how Nature was discovered unto them.

Hereby was that high and noble spirit of Brother C. R. C. so stired up, that Jerusalem was not so much now in his mind as Damasco ;[1] also he could not bridle his desires any longer, but made a bargain with the Arabians that they should carry him for a certain sum of money to Damcar.

He was but of the age of sixteen years when he came thither, yet of a strong Dutch constitution. There the Wise Men received him not as a stranger (as he himself witnesseth), but as one whom they had long expected ; they called him by his name, and shewed him other secrets out of his cloyster, whereat he could not but mightily wonder.

He learned there better the Arabian tongue, so that the year following he translated the book M into good Latin, which he afterwards brought with him, This is the place where he did learn his Physick and his Mathematics, whereof the world hath much cause to rejoice, if there were more love and less envy.

After three years he returned again with good consent, shipped himself over *Sinus Arabicus* into Egypt, where he remained not long, but only took better notice there of the plants and creatures. He sailed over the whole Mediterranean Sea for to come unto Fez, where the Arabians had directed him.

It is a great shame unto us that wise men, so far remote the one from the other, should not only be of one opinion, hating all contentious writings, but also

[1] Damascus and the unknown city denominated Damcar are continually confused in the German editions. Brother C. R. C. evidently did not project a journey to Damascus, which he had already reached ; nevertheless this is the name appearing in this place, and I have decided on retaining it for reasons which will subsequently be made evident.

be so willing and ready, under the seal of secresy, to impart their secrets to others. Every year the Arabians and Africans do send one to another, inquiring one of another out of their arts, if happily they had found out some better things, or if experience had weakened their reasons. Yearly there came something to light whereby the Mathematics, Physic, and Magic (for in those are they of Fez most skilful) were amended. There is now-a-days no want of learned men in Germany, Magicians, Cabalists, Physicians, and Philosophers, were there but more love and kindness among them, or that the most part of them would not keep their secrets close only to themselves.

At Fez he did get acquaintance with those which are commonly called the Elementary inhabitants, who revealed unto him many of their secrets, as we Germans likewise might gather together many things if there were the like unity and desire of searching out secrets amongst us.

Of these of Fez he often did confess, that their Magia was not altogether pure, and also that their Cabala was defiled with their Religion; but, notwith-standing, he knew how to make good use of the same, and found still more better grounds for his faith, altogether agreeable with the harmony of the whole world, and wonderfully impressed in all periods of time. Thence proceedeth that fair Concord, that as in every several kernel is contained a whole good tree or fruit, so likewise is included in the little body of man, the whole great world, whose religion, policy, health, members, nature, language, words, and works, are agreeing, sympathizing, and in equal tune and melody with God, Heaven, and Earth; and that which is disagreeing with them is error, falsehood, and of the devil, who alone is the first, middle, and last cause of strife, blindness, and darkness in the world. Also, might one examine all and several persons upon the earth, he should find that which is good and right is always agreeing with itself, but all the rest is spotted with a thousand erroneous conceits.

After two years Brother R. C. departed the city Fez, and sailed with many costly things into Spain, hoping well, as he himself had so well and profitably spent his time in his travel, that the learned in Europe would highly rejoyce with him, and begin to rule and order all their studies according to those sure and sound foundations. He therefore conferred with the learned in Spain, shewing unto them the errors of our arts, and how they might be corrected, and from whence they should gather the true *Inditia* of the times to come, and wherein they ought to agree with those things that are past; also how the faults of the Church and the whole *Philosophia Moralis* were to be amended. He shewed them new growths, new fruits, and beasts, which did concord with old philosophy, and prescribed them new Axiomata, whereby all things might fully be restored. But it was to them a laughing matter, and being a new thing unto them, they feared that their great name would be lessened if they should now again begin to learn, and acknowledge their many years' errors, to which they were accustomed, and wherewith they had gained them enough. Who so loveth unquietness, let him be reformed (they said). The same song was also sung to him by other nations, the which moved him the more because it happened to him contrary to his expectation, being then ready bountifully to impart all his arts and secrets to the learned, if they would have but undertaken to write the true and infallible Axiomata, out of all faculties, sciences, and arts, and whole nature, as that which he knew would direct them, like a globe or circle, to the onely middle point and *centrum*, and (as it is usual among the Arabians) it should onely serve to the wise and learned for a rule, that also there might be a society in Europe which might have gold, silver, and precious stones, sufficient for to bestow them on kings for their necessary uses and lawful purposes, with which [society] such as be governors might be brought up for to learn all that which God hath suffered man to know, and thereby to be enabled in all times of need to give their counsel unto those that seek it, like the Heathen Oracles.

Verily we must confess that the world in those days was already big with those great commotions, labouring to be delivered of them, and did bring forth painful, worthy men, who brake with all force through darkness and barbarism, and left us who succeeded to follow them. Assuredly they have been the uppermost point in *Trygono igneo*, whose flame now should be more and more brighter, and shall undoubtedly give to the world the last light.

Such a one likewise hath Theophrastus been in vocation and callings, although he was none of our Fraternity, yet, nevertheless hath he diligently read over the Book M, whereby his sharp ingenium was exalted; but this man was also hindered in his course by the multitude of the learned and wise-seeming men, that he was never able peaceably to confer with others of the knowledge and understanding he had of Nature. And therefore in his writings he rather mocked these busie bodies, and doth not shew them altogether what he was; yet, nevertheless, there is found with him well grounded the afore-named Harmonia, which without doubt he had imparted to the learned, if he had not found them rather worthy of subtil vexation then to be instructed in greater arts and sciences. He thus with a free and careless life lost his time, and left unto the world their foolish pleasures.

But that we do not forget our loving Father, Brother C. R., he after many painful travels, and his fruitless true instructions, returned again into Germany, the which he heartily loved, by reason of the alterations which were shortly to come, and of the strange and dangerous contentions. There, although he could have bragged with his art, but specially of the transmutations of metals, yet did he esteem more Heaven, and men, the citizens thereof, than all vain glory and pomp.

Nevertheless, he builded a fitting and neat habitation, in the which he ruminated his voyage and philosophy, and reduced them together in a true memorial. In this house he spent a great time in the mathematics, and made many fine instruments, *ex omnibus hujus artis partibus*, whereof there is but little remaining to us, as hereafter you shall understand.

After five years came again into his mind the wished for Reformation; and in regard [of it] he doubted of the ayd and help of others, although he himself was painful, lusty, and unwearisom; howsoever he undertook, with some few adjoyned with him, to attempt the same. Wherefore he desired to that end to have out of his first cloyster (to the which he bare a great affection) three of his brethren, Brother G. V., Brother I. A., and Brother I. O., who had some more knowledge of the arts than at that time many others had. He did bind those three unto himself, to be faithful, diligent, and secret, as also to commit carefully to writing all that which he should direct and instruct them in, to the end that those which were to come, and through especial revelation should be received into this Fraternity, might not be deceived of the least sillable and word.

After this manner began the Fraternity of the Rosie Cross—first, by four persons onely, and by them was made the magical language and writing, with a large dictionary, which we yet dayly use to God's praise and glory, and do finde great wisdom therein. They made also the first part of the Book M, but in respect that that labour was too heavy, and the unspeakable concourse of the sick hindered them, and also whilst his new building (called *Sancti Spiritus*) was now finished, they concluded to draw and receive yet others more into their Fraternity. To this end was chosen Brother R. C., his deceased father's brother's son; Brother B., a skilful painter; G. G., and P. D., their secretary, all Germans except I. A., so in all they were eight in number, all batchelors and of vowed virginity, by whom was collected a book or volumn of all that which man can desire, wish, or hope for.

Although we do now freely confess that the world is much amended within an hundred years, yet we are assured that our Axiomata shall immovably remain unto the world's end, and also the world in her highest and last age shall not attain to see anything else: for our ROTA takes her beginning from that day when God spake *Fiat* and shall end when he shall speak *Pereat;* yet God's clock striketh every minute, where ours scarce striketh perfect hours. We also stedfastly beleeve, that if our Brethren and Fathers had lived in this our present and clear light, they would more roughly have handled the Pope, Mahomet, scribes, artists, and sophisters, and showed themselves more helpful, not simply with sighs and wishing of their end and consummation.

When now these eight Brethren had disposed and ordered all things in such manner, as there was not now need of any great labour, and also that every one was sufficiently instructed and able perfectly to discourse of secret and manifest philosophy, they would not remain any longer together, but, as in the beginning they had agreed, they separated themselves into several countries, because that not only their Axiomata might in secret be more profoundly examined by the learned, but that they themselves, if in some country or other they observed anything, or perceived some error, might inform one another of it.

Their agreement was this:—

First, That none of them should profess any other thing than to cure the sick, and that gratis.

Second, None of the posterity should be constrained to wear one certain kind of habit, but therein to follow the custom of the country.

Third, That every year, upon the day C., they should meet together at the house *Sancti Spiritus*, or write the cause of his absence.

Fourth, Every Brother should look about for a worthy person who, after his decease, might succeed him.

Fifth, The word R. C. should be their seal, mark, and character.

Sixth, The Fraternity should remain secret one hundred years.

These six articles they bound themselves one to another to keep; five of the Brethren departed, onely the Brethren B. and D. remained with the Father, Brother R. C., a whole year. When these likewise departed, then remained by him his cousen and Brother I. O., so that he hath all the days of his life with him two of his Brethren. And although that as yet the Church was not cleansed, never heless, we know that they did think of her, and what with longing desire they looked for. Every year they assembled together with joy, and made a full resolution of that which they had done. There must certainly have been great pleasure to hear truly and without invention related and rehearsed all the wonders which God hath poured out here and there throughout the world. Every one may hold it out for certain, that such persons as were sent, and joyned together by God and the Heavens, and chosen out of the wisest of men as have lived in many ages, did live together above all others in highest unity, greatest secresy, and most kindness one towards another.

After such a most laudable sort they did spend their lives, but although they were free from all diseases and pain, yet, notwithstanding, they could not live and pass their time appointed of God. The first of this Fraternity which dyed, and that in England, was I. O., as Brother C. long before had foretold him; he was very expert, and well learned in Cabala, as his Book called H witnesseth. In England he is much spoken of, and chiefly because he cured a young Earl of Norfolk of the leprosie. They had concluded, that, as much as possibly could be, their burial place should be kept secret, as at this day it is not known unto us what is become of some of them, yet every one's place was supplied with a fit successor. But this we will confesse publickly by these presents, to the honour of God, that what secret soever we have learned out of the book M, although before our eyes we behold the image and pattern of all the world, yet are there not shewn unto us our misfortunes, nor hour of death, the which only is known to God Himself, who thereby would have us keep in a continual readiness. But hereof more in our Confession, where we do set down thirty-seven reasons wherefore we now do make known our Fraternity, and proffer such high mysteries freely, without constraint and reward. Also we do promise more gold then both the Indies bring to the King of Spain, for Europe is with child, and will bring forth a strong child, who shall stand in need of a great godfather's gift.

After the death of I. O., Brother R. C. rested not, but, as soon as he could, called the rest together, and then, as we suppose, his grave was made, although hitherto we (who were the latest) did not know when our loving Father R. C. died, and had no more but the bare names of the beginners, and all their successors to us. Yet there came into our memory a secret, which, through dark and hidden words and speeches of the hundred years, Brother A., the successor of D. (who was of the last and second row of succession, and had lived amongst many of us), did impart unto us of the third row and succession; otherwise we must confess, that after the death of the said A., none of us had in any manner known anything of Brother C. R., and of his first fellow-brethren, then that which was extant of them in our philosophical BIBLIOTHECA, amongst which our AXIOMATA was held for the chiefest, ROTA MUNDI for the most artificial, and PROTHEUS for the most profitable. Likewise, we do not certainly know if these of the second row have been of like wisdom as the first, and if they were admitted to all things,

It shall be declared hereafter to the gentle reader not onely what we have heard of the burial of Brother R. C., but also it shall be made manifest publicly, by the foresight, sufferance, and commandment of God, whom we most faithfully obey, that if we shall be answered discreetly and Christian-like, we will not be ashamed to set forth publickly in print our names and surnames, our meetings, or anything else that may be required at our hands.

Now, the true and fundamental relation of the finding out of the high-illuminated man of God, *Fra: C. R. C.*, is this:—After that A. in *Gallia Narbonensi* was deceased, there succeeded in his place our loving Brother N. N. This man, after he had repaired unto us to take the solemn oath of fidelity and secresy, informed us *bona fide*, that A. had comforted him in telling him, that this Fraternity should ere long not remain so hidden, but should be to all the whole German nation helpful, needful, and commendable, of the which he was not in anywise in his estate ashamed. The year following, after he had performed his school right, and was minded now to travel, being for that purpose sufficiently provided with Fortunatus' purse, he thought (he being a good architect) to alter something of his building, and to make it more fit. In such renewing, he lighted upon the Memorial Table, which was cast of brasse, and containeth all the names of the Brethren, with some few other things. This he would transfer into another more fitting vault, for where or when Brother R. C. died, or in what country he was buried, was by our predecessors concealed and unknown unto us. In this table stuck a great naile somewhat strong, so that when it was with force drawn out it took with it an indifferent big stone out of the thin wall or plaistering of the hidden door, and so unlooked for uncovered the door, whereat we did with joy and longing throw down the rest of the wall and cleared the door, upon which was written in great letters—

Post CXX Annos Patebo,

with the year of the Lord under it. Therefore we gave God thanks, and let it rest that same night, because first we would overlook our *Rota*—but we refer ourselves again to the Confession, for what we here publish is done for the help of those that are worthy, but to the unworthy, God willing, it will be small profit. For like as our door was after so many years wonderfully discovered, also there shall be opened a door to Europe (when the wall is removed), which already doth begin to appear, and with great desire is expected of many.

In the morning following we opened the door, and there appeared to our sight a vault of seven sides and seven corners, every side five foot broad, and the height of eight foot. Although the sun never shined in this vault, nevertheless, it was enlightened with another sun, which had learned this from the sun, and was situated in the upper part in the center of the sieling. In the midst, instead of a tomb-stone, was a round altar, covered with a plate of brass, and thereon this engraven :—

A. C. R. C. *Hoc universi compendium unius mihi sepulchrum feci.*

Round about the first circle or brim stood,

Jesus mihi omnia.

In the middle were four figures, inclosed in circles, whose circumscription was,

1. *Nequaquam Vacuum.*
2. *Legis Jugum.*
3. *Libertas Evangelii.*
4. *Dei Gloria Intacta.*

This is all clear and bright, as also the seventh side and the two heptagons. So we kneeled down altogether, and gave thanks to the sole wise, sole mighty, and sole eternal God, who hath taught us more than all men's wits could have found out, praised be His holy name. This vault we parted in three parts, the upper part or sieling, the wall or side, the ground or floor. Of the upper part you shall understand no more at this time but that it was divided according to the seven sides in the triangle which was in the bright center; but what therein is contained you (that are desirous of our Society) shall, God willing, behold the same with your own eyes. Every side or wall is parted into ten squares, every one with their several figures and sentences,, as they are truly shewed and set forth *concentratum* here in our book. The bottom again is parted in the triangle, but because therein is described the power and rule of the Inferior Governors, we leave to manifest the same, for fear of the abuse by the evil and ungodly world. But those that are provided and stored with the Heavenly Antidote, do without fear or hurt, tread on and bruise the head of the old and evil serpent, which this our age is well fitted for. Every side or wall had a door for a chest, wherein there lay divers things, especially all our books, which otherwise we had, besides the *Vocabulario* of Theophrastus Paracelsus of Hohenheim, and these which daily unfalsifieth we do participate. Herein also we found his *Itinerarium* and *Vita*, whence this relation for the most part is taken. In another chest were looking-glasses of divers virtues, as also in other places were little bells, burning lamps, and chiefly wonderful artificial songs—generally all was done to that end, that if it should happen, after many hundred years, the Fraternity should come to nothing, they might by this onely vault be restored again.

Now, as we had not yet seen the dead body of our careful and wise Father, we therefore removed the altar aside; then we lifted up a strong plate of brass, and found a fair and worthy body, whole and unconsumed, as the same is here lively counterfeited,[1] with all the ornaments and attires. In his hand he held a parchment called T.[2] the which next unto the Bible is our greatest treasure, which ought not to be delivered to the censure of the world. At the end of this book standeth this following *Elogium.*

Granum pectori Jesu insitum.

C. R. C. ex nobili atque splendida Germaniæ R. C. familia oriundus, vir sui seculi divinis revelationibus, subtilissimis imaginationibus, indefessis laboribus ad cœslestia atque humana mysteria; arcanavè admissus postquam suam (quam Arabico at Africano itineribus collejerat) plus quam regiam, atque imperatoriam Gazam suo seculo nondum convenientem, posteritati eruendam custodivisset et jam suarum Artium, ut et nominis, fides ac conjunctissimos heredes instituisset, mundum minutum omnibus motibus magno illi respondentem fabricasset hocque tandem preteritarum, præsentium, et futurarum, rerum compendio extracto, centenario major, non morbo (quem ipse nunquam corpore expertus erat, nunquam alios infestare sinebat) ullo pellente sed Spiritis Dei evocante, illuminatam animam (inter Fratrum amplexus et ultima oscula) fidelissimo Creatori Deo reddi-

---

[1] The illustration which is here referred to is, singularly enough, not reproduced in the text of the translation, and it is also absent from the Dutch version of 1617. As there are no other editions of the "Fama Fraternitatis" in the Library of the British Museum, I also am unable to gratify the curiosity of my readers by a copy of the original engraving.

[2] In the English translation the letter I has been substituted by a typographical error, or by an error of transcription for the T which is found in all the Geman editions.

disset, Pater delictissimus, Frater suavissimus, præceptor fidelissimus, amicus integerimus, a suis ad 120 annos hic absconditus est.

Underneath they had subscribed themselves,

1. *Fra. I. A. Fra. C. H. electione Fraternitatis caput.*
2. *Fra. G. V. M. P. C.*
3. *Fra. F. R. C., Junior haeres S. Spiritus.*
4. *Fra. F. B. M. P. A., Pictor et Architectus.*
5. *Fra. G. G. M. P. I., Cabalista.*

Secundi Circuli.

1. *Fra. P. A. Successor, Fra. I. O., Mathematicus.*
2. *Fra. A. Successor, Fra. P. D.*
3. *Fra. R. Successor Patris C. R. C., cum Christo triumphantis.*

At the end was written,

Ex Deo nascimur, in Jesu morimur, per Spiritum Sanctum reviviscimus.

At that time was already dead, Brother I. O. and Brother D., but their burial place where is it to be found? We doubt not but our *Fra. Senior* hath the same, and some especial thing layd in earth, and perhaps likewise hidden. We also hope that this our example will stir up others more diligently to enquire after their names (which we have therefore published), and to search for the place of their burial; the most part of them, by reason of their practice and physick, are yet known and praised among very old folks; so might perhaps our GAZA be enlarged, or, at least, be better cleared.

Concerning *Minutum Mundum*, we found it kept in another little altar, truly more finer then can be imagined by any understanding man, but we will leave him undescribed untill we shall be truly answered upon this our true-hearted FAMA. So we have covered it again with the plates, and set the altar thereon, shut the door and made it sure with all our seals. Moreover, by instruction, and command of our ROTA, there are come to sight some books, among which is contained M (which were made instead of household care by the praiseworthy M. P.). Finally, we departed the one from the other, and left the natural heirs in possession of our jewels. And so we do expect the answer and judgment of the learned and unlearned.

Howbeit we know after a time there will now be a general reformation, both of divine and humane things, according to our desire and the expectation of others; for it is fitting, that before the rising of the Sun there should appear and break forth *Aurora*, or some clearness, or divine light in the sky. And so, in the meantime, some few, which shall give their names, may joyn together, thereby to increase the number and respect of our Fraternity, and make a happy and wished for beginning of our PHILOSOPHICAL CANONS, prescribed to us by our Brother R. C., and he partakers with us of our treasures (which never can fail or be wasted) in all humility and love, to be eased of this world's labours, and not walk so blindly in the knowledge of the wonderful works of God.

But that also every Christian may know of what Religion and belief we are, we confess to have the knowledge of Jesus Christ (as the same now in these last days, and chiefly in Germany, most clear and pure is professed, and is now adays cleansed and voyd of all swerving people, hereticks, and false prophets), in certain and noted countries maintained, defended, and propagated. Also we use two Sacraments, as they are instituted with all Formes and Ceremonies of the first and renewed Church. In *Politia* we acknowledge the Roman Empire and *Quartam Monarchiam* for our Christian head, albeit we know what alterations be at hand, and would fain impart the same with all our hearts to other godly learned men, notwithstanding our handwriting which is in our hands, no man (except God alone) can make it common, nor any unworthy person is able to bereave us of it. But we shall help with secret aid this so good a cause, as God shall permit or hinder us. For our God is not blinde, as the heathen's Fortuna, but is the Churches' ornament and the honour of the Temple. Our Philosophy also is not a new invention, but as Adam after his fall hath received it, and as Moses and Solomon used it, also it ought not much to be doubted of, or contradicted by other opinions, or meanings; but seeing the truth is peaceable, brief, and always like herself in all things, and especially accorded by with *Jesus in omni parte* and all members, and as He is the true image of the Father, so is she His image, so it shal not be said, This is true according to Philosophy, but true according to Theologie; and wherein Plato, Aristotle, Pythagoras, and others did hit the mark, and wherein Enoch, Abraham, Moses, Solomon, did excel, but especially wherewith that wonderful book the Bible agreeth. All that same concurreth together, and maketh a sphere or globe whose total parts, are equidistant from the center, as hereof more at large and more plain shal be spoken of in Christianly Conference (in den Boecke des Levens).

But now concerning, and chiefly in this our age, the ungodly and accursed gold-making, which hath gotten so much the upper hand, whereby under colour of it, many runagates and roguish people do use great villainies, and cozen and abuse the credit which is given them; yea, now adays men of discretion do hold the transmutation of metals to be the highest point and *fastigium* in philosophy. This is all their intent and desire, and that God would be more esteemed by them and honoured which could make great store of gold, the which with unpremeditate prayers they hope to obtain of the alknowing God and searcher of all hearts; but we by these presents publickly testifie, that the true philosophers are far of another minde, esteeming little the making of gold, which is but a *paragon*, for besides that they have a thousand better things. We say with our loving Father C. R. C., *Phy. aurium nisi quantum aurum*, for unto him the whole nature is detected; he doth not rejoice that he can make gold, and that, as saith Christ, the devils are obedient unto him, but is glad that he seeth the Heavens open, the angels of God ascending and descending, and his name written in the book of life.

Also we do testifie that, under the name of *Chymia*, many books and pictures are set forth in *Contumeliam gloriae Dei*, as we wil name them in their due season, and wil give to the pure-hearted a catalogue or register of them. We pray all learned men to take heed of these kinde of books, for the Enemy never resteth, but soweth his weeds til a stronger one doth root them out.

So, according to the wil and meaning of *Fra.* C. R. C., we his brethren request again all the learned in Europe who shal read (sent forth in five languages) this our *Fama* and *Confessio*, that it would please them with good deliberation to ponder this our offer, and to examine most nearly and sharply their arts, and behold the present time with all diligence, and to declare their minde, either *communicato consilio*, or *singulatim* by print. And although at this time we make no mention either of our names or meetings, yet nevertheless every one's opinion shal assuredly come to our hands, in what language so ever it be, nor any body shal fail, whoso gives but his name, to speak with some of us, either by word of mouth, or else, if there be some lett, in writing. And this we say for a truth, that whosoever shal earnestly, and from his heart, bear affection unto us, it shal be beneficial to him in goods, body, and soul; but he that is false-hearted, or onely greedy of riches, the same first of all shal not be able in any manner of wise to hurt us, but bring himself to utter ruine and destruction. Also our building, although one hundred thousand people had very near seen and beheld the same, shal for ever remain untouched, undestroyed, and hidden to the wicked world.

Sub umbra alarum tuarum, Jehova.

Confessio.

———

THE translation of this manifesto which follows the Fama in the edition accredited by the great name of Eugenius Philalethes is prolix and careless: being made not from the Latin original but from the later German version. As a relic of English Rosicrucian literature I have wished to preserve it, and having subjected it to a searching revision throughout, it now represents the original with sufficient fidelity for all practical purposes. The "Confessio Fraternitatis" appeared in the year 1615 in a Latin work entitled "Secretioris Philosophiæ Consideratio Brevio à Philippo à Gabella, Philosophiæ studisso, conscripta ; et nunc primum unà cum Confessione Fraternitatis R. C.," in lucem edita, Cassellis, excudebat G. Wesselium, a 1615. Quarto." It was prefaced by the following advertisement :—

"Here, gentle reader, you shall find incorporated in our Confession thirty-seven reasons of our purpose and intention, the which according to thy pleasure thou mayst seek out and compare together, considering within thyself if they be sufficient to allure thee. Verily, it requires no small pains to induce any one to believe what doth not yet appear, but when it shall be revealed in the full blaze of day, I suppose we should be ashamed of such questionings. And as we do now securely call the Pope Antichrist, which was formerly a capital offence in every place, so we know certainly that what we here keep secret we shall in the future thunder forth with uplifted voice, the which, reader, with us desire with all thy heart that it may happen most speedily.   "FRATRES R. C."

Confessio Fraternitatis R. C. ad Eruditos Europae.

CHAPTER I.

Whatsoever you have heard, O mortals, concerning our Fraternity by the trumpet sound of the Fama R. C., do not either believe it hastily, or wilfully suspect it. It is Jehovah who, seeing how the world is falling to decay, and near to its end, doth hasten it again to its beginning, inverting the course of Nature, and so what heretofore hath been sought with great pains and dayly labor He doth lay open now to those thinking of no such thing, offering it to the willing and thrusting it on the reluctant, that it may become to the good that which will smooth the troubles of human life and break the violence of unexpected blows of Fortune, but to the ungodly that which will augment their sins and their punishments.

Although we believe ourselves to have sufficiently unfolded to you in the *Fama* the nature of our order, wherein we follow the will of our most excellent father, nor can by any be suspected of heresy, nor of any attempt against the commonwealth, we hereby do condemn the East and the West (meaning the Pope and Mahomet) for their blasphemies against our Lord Jesus Christ, and offer to the chief head of the Roman Empire our prayers, secrets, and great treasures of gold. Yet we have thought good for the sake of the learned to add somewhat more to this, and make a better explanation, if there be anything too deep, hidden, and set down over dark, in the Fama, or for certain reasons altogether omitted, whereby we hope the learned will be more addicted unto us, and easier to approve our counsel.

CHAPTER II.

Concerning the amendment of philosophy, we have (as much as at this present is needful) declared that the same is altogether weak and faulty; nay, whilst many (I know not how) alledge that she is sound and strong, to us it is certain that she fetches her last breath.

But as commonly even in the same place where there breaketh forth a new disease, nature discovereth a remedy against the same, so amidst so many infirmities of philosophy there do appear the right means, and unto our Fatherland sufficiently offered, whereby she may become sound again, and new or renovated may appear to a renovated world.

No other philosophy we have then that which is the head of all the faculties, sciences, and arts, the which (if we behold our age) containeth much of Theology and Medicine, but little of Jurisprudence; which searcheth heaven and earth with exquisite analysis, or, to speak briefly thereof, which doth sufficiently manifest the Microsums man, whereof if some of the more orderly in the number of the learned shall respond to our fraternal invitation, they shall find among us far other and greater wonders then those they heretofore did believe, marvel at, and profess.

CHAPTER III.

Wherefore, to declare briefly our meaning hereof, it becomes us to labor carefully that the surprise of our challenge may be taken from you, to shew plainly that such secrets are not lightly esteemed by us, and not to spread an opinion abroad among the vulgar that the story concerning them is a foolish thing. For it is not absurd to suppose many are overwhelmed with the conflict of thought which is occasioned by our unhoped graciousness, unto whom (as yet) be unknown the wonders of the sixth age, or who, by reason of the course of the world, esteem the things to come like unto the present, and, hindered by the obstacles of their age, live no otherwise in the world then as men blind, who, in the light of noon, discern nothing onely by feeling.

CHAPTER IV.

Now concerning the first part, we hold that the meditations of our Christian father on all subjects which from the creation of the world have been invented, brought forth, and propagated by human ingenuity, through God's revelation, or through the service of Angels or spirits, or through the sagacity of understanding, or through the experience of long observation, are so great, that if all books should perish, and by God's almighty sufferance all writings and all learning should be lost, yet posterity will be able thereby to lay a new foundation of sciences, and to erect a new citadel of truth; the which perhaps would not be so hard to do as if one should begin to pull down and destroy the old, ruinous building, then enlarge the fore-court, afterwards bring light into the private chambers, and then change the doors, staples, and other things according to our intention.

Therefore, it must not be expected that new comers shall attain at once all our weighty secrets. They must proceed step by step from the smaller to the greater, and must not be retarded by difficulties.

Wherefore should we not freely acquiesce in the onely truth then seek through so many windings and labyrinths, if onely it had pleased God to lighten unto us the sixth Candelabrum? Were it not sufficient for us to fear neither hunger, poverty, diseases, nor age? Were it not an excellent thing to live always so as if you had lived from the beginning of the world, and should still live to the end thereof? So to live in one place that neither the people which dwel beyond the Ganges could hide anything, nor those which live in Peru might be able to keep secret their counsels from thee? So to read in one onely book as to discern, understand, and remember whatsoever in all other books (which heretofore have been, are now, and hereafter shal come out) hath been, is, and shal be learned out of them? So to sing or to play that instead of stony rocks you could draw pearls, instead of wild beasts spirits, and instead of Pluto you could soften the mighty princes of the world? O mortals, diverse is the counsel of God and your convenience, Who hath decreed at this time to encrease and enlarge the number of our Fraternity, the which we with such joy have undertaken, as we have heretofore obtained this great treasure without our merits, yea, without any hope or expectation; the same we purpose with such fidelity to put in practice, that neither compassion nor pity for our own children (which some of us in the Fraternity have) shal move us, since we know that these unhoped for good things cannot be inherited, nor be conferred promiscuously.

<h3 style="text-align:center">CHAPTER V.</h3>

If there be any body now which on the other side wil complain of our discretion, that we offer our treasures so freely and indiscriminately, and do not rather regard more the godly, wise, or princely persons then the common people, with him we are in no wise angry (for the accusation is not without moment), but withall we affirm that we have by no means made common property of our arcana, albeit they resound in five languages within the ears of the vulgar, both because, as we well know, they will not move gross wits, and because the worth of those who shal be accepted into our Fraternity will not be measured by their curiosity, but by the rule and pattern of our revelations. A thousand times the unworthy may clamour, a thousand times may present themselves, yet God hath commanded our ears that they should hear none of them, and hath so compassed us about with His clouds that unto us, His servants, no violence can be done; wherefore now no longer are we beheld by human eyes, unless they have received strength borrowed from the eagle.

For the rest, it hath been necessary that the Fama should be set forth in everyone's mother tongue, lest those should not be defrauded of the knowledge thereof, whom (although they be unlearned) God hath not excluded from the happiness of this Fraternity, which is divided into degrees; as those which dwell in Damcar, who have a far different politick order from the other Arabians; for there do govern onely understanding men, who, by the king's permission, make particular laws, according unto which example the government shall also be instituted in Europe (according to the description set down by our Christianly Father), when that shal come to pass which must precede, when our Trumpet shall resound with full voice and with no prevarications of meaning, when, namely, those things of which a few now whisper and darken with enigmas, shall openly fill the earth, even as after many secret chafings of pious people against the pope's tyranny, and after timid reproof, he with great violence and by a great onset was cast down from his seat and abundantly trodden under foot, whose final fall is reserved for an age when he shall be torn in pieces with nails, and a final groan shall end his ass's braying, the which, as we know, is already manifest to many learned men in Germany, as their tokens and secret congratulations bear witness.

<h3 style="text-align:center">CHAPTER VI.</h3>

We could here relate and declare what all the time from the year 1378 (when our Christian father was born) till now hath happened, what alterations he hath seen in the world these one hundred and six years of his life, what he left after his happy death to be attempted by our Fathers and by us, but brevity, which we do observe, will not permit at this present to make rehearsal of it; it is enough for those which do not despise our declaration to have touched upon it, thereby to prepare the way for their more close union and association with us. Truly, to whom it is permitted to behold, read, and thenceforward teach himself those great characters which the Lord God hath inscribed upon the world's mechanism, and which He repeats through the mutations of Empires, such an one is already ours, though as yet unknown to himself; and as we know he will not neglect our invitation, so, in like manner, we abjure all deceit, for we promise that no man's uprightness and hopes shall deceive him who shall make himself known to us under the seal of secrecy and desire our familiarity. But to the false and to impostors, and to those who seek other things then wisdom, we witness by these presents publickly, we cannot be betrayed unto them to our hurt, nor be known to them without the will of God, but they shall certainly be partakers of that terrible commination spoken of in our Fama, and their impious designs shall fall back upon their own heads, while our treasures shall remain untouched, till the Lion shall arise and exact them as his right, receive and imploy them for the establishment of his kingdom.

CHAPTER VII.

One thing should here, O mortals, be established by us, that God hath decreed to the world before her end, which presently thereupon shall ensue, an influx of truth, light, and grandeur, such as he commanded should accompany Adam from Paradise and sweeten the misery of man: Wherefore there shall cease all falsehood, darkness, and bondage, which little by little, with the great globe's revolution, hath crept into the arts, works, and governments of men, darkening the greater part of them. Thence hath proceeded that innumerable diversity of persuasions, falsities, and heresies, which make choice difficult to the wisest men, seeing on the one part they were hindered by the reputation of philosophers and on the other by the facts of experience, which if (as we trust) it can be once removed, and instead thereof a single and self-same rule be instituted, then there will indeed remain thanks unto them which have taken pains therein, but the sum of the so great work shall be attributed to the blessedness of our age.

As we now confess that many high intelligences by their writings will be a great furtherance unto this Reformation which is to come, so do we by no means arrogate to ourselves this glory, as if such a work were onely imposed on us, but we testify with our Saviour Christ, that sooner shall the stones rise up and offer their service, then there shall be any want of executors of God's counsel.

CHAPTER VIII.

God, indeed, hath already sent messengers which should testifie His will, to wit, some new stars which have appeared in *Serpentarius* and *Cygnus*, the which powerful signs of a great Council shew forth how for all things which human ingenuity discovers, God calls upon His hidden knowledge, as likewise the Book of Nature, though it stands open truly for all eyes, can be read or understood by only a very few.

As in the human head there are two organs of hearing, two of sight, and two of smell, but onely one of speech, and it were but vain to expect speech from the ears, or hearing from the eyes, so there have been ages which have seen, others which have heard, others again that have smelt and tasted. Now, there remains that in a short and swiftly approaching time honour should be likewise given to the tongue, that what formerly saw, heard, and smelt shall finally speak, after the world shall have slept away the intoxication of her poisoned and stupefying chalice, and with an open heart, bare head, and naked feet shall merrily and joyfully go forth to meet the sun rising in the morning.

CHAPTER IX.

These characters and letters, as God hath here and there incorporated them in the Sacred Scriptures, so hath He imprinted them most manifestly on the wonderful work of creation, on the heavens, the earth, and on all beasts, so that as the mathematician predicts eclipses, so we prognosticate the obscurations of the church, and how long they shall last. From these letters we have borrowed our magick writing, and thence have made for ourselves a new language, in which the nature of things is expressed, so that it is no wonder that we are not so eloquent in other tongues, least of all in this Latin, which we know to be by no means in agreement with that of Adam and of Enoch, but to have been contaminated by the confusion of Babel.[1]

CHAPTER X.

But this also must by no means be omitted, that, while there are yet some eagle's feathers in our way, the which do hinder our purpose, we do exhort to the sole, onely, assiduous, and continual study of the Sacred Scriptures, for he that taketh all his pleasures therein shall know that he hath prepared for himself an excellent way to come into our Fraternity, for this is the whole sum of our Laws, that as there is not a character in that great miracle of the world which has not a claim on the memory, so those are nearest and likest unto us who do make the Bible the rule of their life, the end of all their studies, and the compendium of the universal world, from whom we require not that it should be continually in their mouth, but that they should appropriately apply its true interpretation to all ages of the world, for it is not our custom so to debase the divine oracle, that while there are innumerable expounders of the same, some adhere to the opinions of their party, some make sport of Scripture as if it were a tablet of wax to be indifferently made use of by theologians, philosophers, doctors, and mathematicians. Be it ours rather to bear witness, that from the beginning of the world there hath not been given to man a more excellent, admirable, and wholesome book then the Holy Bible; Blessed is he who possesses it, more blessed is he who reads it, most blessed of all is he who truly understandeth it, while he is most like to God who both understands and obeys it.

CHAPTER XI.

Now, whatsoever hath been said in the Fama, through hatred of impostors, against the transmutation of metals and the supreme medicine of the world, we desire to be so understood, that this so great gift of God we do in no manner set at naught, but as it bringeth not always with it the knowledge of Nature, while this knowledge bringeth forth both that and an infinite number of other natural miracles, it is right that we be rather earnest to attain to the knowledge of philosophy, nor tempt excellent wits to the tincture of metals sooner then to the observation of Nature. He must needs be insariable to whom neither poverty, disease, nor danger can any longer reach, who, as one raised above all men, hath rule over that which doth anguish, afflict, and pain others, yet will give himself again to idle things, will build, make wars, and domineer, because he hath gold sufficient, and of silver an inexhaustible fountain. God judgeth far otherwise, who exalteth the lowly, and casteth the proud into obscurity; to the silent he sendeth his angels to hold speech with them, but the babblers he driveth into the wilderness, which is the judgment due to the Roman impostor who now poureth his blasphemies with open mouth against Christ, nor yet in the full light, by which Germany hath detected his caves and subterranean passages, will abstain from lying, that thereby he may fulfil the measure of his sin, and be found worthy of the axe. Therefore, one day it will come to pass, that the mouth of this viper shall be stopped, and his triple crown shall be brought to nought, of which things more fully when we shall have met together.

CHAPTER XII.

For conclusion of our Confession we must earnestly admonish you, that you cast away, if not all, yet most of the worthless books of pseudo chymists, to whom it is a jest to apply the Most Holy Trinity to vain things, or to deceive men with monstrous symbols and enigmas, or to profit by the curiosity of the credulous; our age doth produce many such, one of the greatest being a stage-player, a man with sufficient ingenuity for imposition; such doth the enemy of human welfare mingle among the good seed, thereby to make the truth more difficult to be believed, which in herself is simple and naked, while falsehood is

[1] The original reads *Babylonis confusione,* "by the confusion of Babylon."

proud, haughty, and coloured with a lustre of seeming godly and humane wisdom. Ye that are wise eschew such books, and have recourse to us, who seek not your moneys, but offer unto you most willingly our great treasures. We hunt not after your goods with invented lying tinctures, but desire to make you partakers of our goods. We do not reject parables, but invite you to the clear and simple explanation of all secrets : we seek not to be received of you, but call you unto our more then kingly houses and palaces, by no motion of our own, but (lest you be ignorant of it) as forced thereto by the Spirit of God, commanded by the testament of our most excellent Father, and impelled by the occasion of this present time.

CHAPTER XIII.

What think you, therefore, O Mortals, seeing that we sincerely confess Christ, execrate the pope, addict ourselves to the true philosophy, lead a worthy life, and dayly call, intreat, and invite many more unto our Fraternity, unto whom the same Light of God likewise appeareth? Consider you not that, having pondered the gifts which are in you, having measured your understanding in the Word of God, and having weighed the imperfection and inconsistencies of all the arts, you may at length in the future deliberate with us upon their remedy, co-operate in the work of God, and be serviceable to the constitution of your time? On which work these profits will follow, that all those goods when Nature hath dispersed in every part of the earth shall at one time and altogether be given to you, *tanquam in centro solis et lunge*. Then shall you be able to expel from the world all those things which darken human knowledge and hinder action, such as the vain (astronomical) epicycles and eccentric circles.

CHAPTER XIV.

You, however, for whom it is enough to be serviceable out of curiosity to any ordinance, or who are dazzled by the glistering of gold, or who, though now upright, might be led away by such unexpected great riches into an effeminate, idle, luxurious, and pompous life, do not disturb our sacred silence by your clamour, but think, that although there be a medicine which might fully cure all diseases, yet those whom God wishes to try or to chastise shall not be abetted by such an opportunity, so that if we were able to enrich and instruct the whole world, and liberate it from innumerable hardships, yet shall we never be manifested unto any man unless God should favor it, yea, it shall be so far from him who thinks to be partaker of our riches against the will of God that he shall sooner lose his life in seeking us, then attain happiness by finding us.

FRATERNITAS R. C.

The Chymical Marriage of Christian Rosencreutz.

THE whole Rosicrucian controversy centres in this publication, which Buhle describes as "a comic romance of extraordinary talent." It was the first published at Strasbourg in the year 1916, but, as will be seen in the seventh chapter, it is supposed to have existed in manuscript as early as 1601-2, thus antedating by a long period the other Rosicrucian books. Two editions of the German original are preserved in the Library of the British Museum, both bearing the date 1616.[1] It was translated into English for the first time in 1690, under the title of "The Hermetic Romance: or The Chymical Wedding. Written in High Dutch by Christian Rosencreutz. Translated by E. Foxcroft, late Fellow of King's Colledge in Cambridge. Licensed and entered according to Order. Printed by A. Sowle, at the Crooked Billet in Holloway-Lane, Shoreditch; and Sold at the Three-Keys in Nags-Head-Court, Grace-church-street." It is this translation in substance, that is, compressed by the omission of all irrelevant matter and dispensable prolixities, which I now offer to the reader.

The Chymical Marriage of Christian Rosencreutz. Anno 1459.
Arcana publicata vilescunt, et gratiam prophanata amittunt.
Ergo: ne Margaritas objice porcis, seu Asino substernere rosas.

THE FIRST BOOK.

The First Day.

On an evening before Easter-day, I sate at a table, and having in my humble prayer conversed with my Creator and considered many great mysteries (whereof the Father of Lights had shewn me not a few), and being now ready to prepare my heart, together with my dear Paschal Lamb, a small, unleavened, undefiled cake, all on a sudden ariseth so horrible a tempest, that I imagined no other but that, through its mighty force, the hill whereon my little house was founded would fly all in pieces. But inasmuch as this, and the like, from the devil (who had done me

Meditatio.

[1] "Chymische Hochzeit: Christiani Rosencreutz. Anno 1459. Erstlick Gedrucktzor Strasbourg. Anno M.DC.XVI." The second edition was printed by Conrad Echer.

Praeconissa.

many a spight) was no new thing to me, I took courage, and persisted in my meditation till somebody touched me on the back, whereupon I was so hugely terrified that I durst hardly look about me, yet I shewed myself as cheerful as humane frailty would permit. Now the same thing still twitching me several times by the coat. I glanced back and behold it was a fair and glorious lady, whose garments were all skye-colour, and curiously bespangled with golden stars. In her right hand she bare a trumpet of beaten gold, whereon a Name was ingraven which I could well read but am forbidden as yet to reveal. In her left hand she had a great bundle of letters in all languages, which she(as I afterwards understood) was to carry into all countries. She had also large and beautiful wings, full of eyes throughout, wherewith she could mount aloft, and flye swifter than any eagle. As soon as I turned about, she looked through her letters, and at length drew out a small one, which, with great reverence she laid upon the table, and, without one word, departed from me. But in her mounting upward, she gave so mighty a blast on her gallant trumpet that the whole hill echoed thereof, and for a full quarter of an hour afterward I could hardly hear my own words.

Epistola.

In so unlooked for an adventure I was at a loss how to advise myself, and, therefore, fell upon my knees, and besought my Creator to permit nothing contrary to my eternal happiness to befall me, whereupon, with fear and trembling, I went to the letter, which was now so heavy as almost to outweigh gold. As I was diligently viewing it, I found a little Seal, whereupon was ingraven a curious

Sigillum.

Cross, with this inscription In Hoc Signo ☿ Vinces

As soon as I espied this sign I was comforted, not being ignorant that it was little acceptable, and much less useful, to the devil. Whereupon I tenderly opened the letter, and within it, in an azure field, in golden letters, found the following verses written:—

> "This day, this day, this, this
> The Royal Wedding is.
> Art thou thereto by birth inclined,
> And unto joy of Gold design'd?
> Then may'st thou to the mountain tend
> Whereon three stately Temples stand,
> And there see all from end to end.
> Keep watch and ward,
> Thyself regard;
> Unless with diligence thou bathe,
> The Wedding can't thee harmless save:
> He'll damage have that here delays:
> Let him beware too light that weighs."

Underneath stood *Sponsus* and *Sponsa*.

De Nuptiis.

As soon as I read this letter, I was like to have fainted away, all my hair stood on end, and cold sweat trickled down my whole body. For although I well perceived that this was the appointed wedding whereof seven years before I was acquainted in a bodily vision, and which I had with great earnestness attended, and which, lastly, by the account and calculation of the plannets, I found so to be, yet could I never fore-see that it must happen under so grievous and perilous conditions. For whereas I before imagined that to be a well-come guest, I needed onely to appear at the wedding, I was now directed to Divine Providence, of which

Requisita in hospitibus Secundum, 7. Pondera.

until this time I was never certain. I also found, the more I examined myself, that in my head there was onely gross misunderstanding, and blindness in mysterious things, so that I was not able to comprehend even those things which lay under my feet, and which I daily conversed with, much less that I should be born to the searching out and understanding of the secrets of Nature, since, in my opinion, Nature might everywhere find a more vertuous disciple, to whom to intrust her precious, though temporary and changeable treasures. I found also that my bodily behaviour, outward conversation, and brotherly love toward my neighbour was not duly purged and cleansed. Moreover, the tickling of the flesh manifested itself, whose affection was bent only to pomp, bravery, and worldly pride, not to the good of mankind; and I was always contriving how by this art I might in a short time abundantly increase my advantage, rear stately palaces, make myself an everlasting name, and other the like carnal designs. But the obscure words concerning the three Temples did particularly afflict me, which I was not able to make out by any after-speculation. Thus sticking between hope and fear, examining myself again and again, and finding only my own frailty and impotency, and exceedingly amazed at the fore-mentioned threatening, at length I betook myself to my usual course. After I had finished my most fervent prayer, I laid me down in my bed, that so perchance my good angel by the Divine permission might appear, and (as it had formerly happened) instruct me in this affair, which, to the praise of God, did now likewise fall out. For I was yet scarce asleep when me-thought I, together with a numberless multitude of men, lay fettered with great chains in a dark dungeon, wherein we swarmed like bees one over another, and thus rendered each other's affliction more grievous. But although neither I, nor any of the rest, could see one jot, yet I continually heard one heaving himself above the other, when his chains or fetters were become ever so little lighter. Now as I with the rest had continued a good while in this affliction, and each was still reproaching the other with his blindness and captivity, at length we heard many trumpets sounding together, and kettle-drums beating so artificially thereto, that it rejoyced us even in our calamity.

During this noise the cover of the dungeon was lifted up, and a little light let down unto us. Then first might truly have been discerned the bustle we kept, for all went pesle-mesle, and he who perchance had too much heaved up himself and was forced down again under the others' feet. In brief, each one strove to be uppermost, neither did I linger, but, with my weighty fetters, slipt from under the rest, and then heaved myself upon a Stone; howbeit, I was several times caught at by others, from whom, as well as I might, I guarded myself with hands and feet. We imagined that we should all be set at liberty, which yet fell out quite otherwise, for after the nobles who looked upon us through the hole had recreated themselves with our struggling, a certain hoary-headed man called to us to be quiet, and, having obtained it, began thus to say on:

> If wretched mortals would forbear
>   Themselves to so uphold,
> Then sure on them much good confer
>   My righteous Mother would:
> But since the same will not insue,
> They must in care and sorrow rue,
>   And still in prison lie.

1. Electio
incerta.

2. Inscitia
Ignorantia
cæcitas
mentis.

3, 4. Naturæ
secreta.
5, 6.

Mundana
affectio.

Preces.

Visio per-
somnium.

Turris
Cæcitas.

Illustratio.

Magister
carceris.

Vide S.
Bernard,
Serm. 3, de 7
Fragmentis.

> Howbeit, my dear Mother will
>   Their follies over-see,
> Her choicest goods permitting still
>   Too much in Light to be.
> Wherefore, in honour of the feast
>   We this day solemnize,
> That so her grace may be increast,
>   A good deed she'll devise;
> For now a cord shall be let down,
> And whosoe'er can hang thereon
>   Shall freely be releast.

He had scarce done speaking when an Antient Matron commanded her servants to let down the cord seven times into the dungeon, and draw up whomsoever could hang upon it. Good God! that I could sufficiently describe the hurry that arose amongst us; every one strove to reach the cord, and only hindered each other. After seven minutes a little bell rang, whereupon at the

Prima
vectura.

first pull the servants drew up four. At that time I could not come near the cord, having to my huge misfortune betaken myself to the stone at the wall, whereas the cord descended in the middle.

Secunda.

The cord was let down the second time, but divers, because their chains were too heavy, and their hands too tender, could not keep hold on it, and brought down others who else might have held on fast enough. Nay, many were forcibly pulled off by those who could not themselves get at it, so envious were we even in this misery. But they of all most moved my compassion whose weight was so heavy that they tore their hands from their bodies and yet could not get up. Thus it came to pass that at these five times very few were drawn up, for, as soon as the sign was given, tumbled one upon another. Whereupon, the greatest part, and the servants were so nimble at the draught that the most part even myself, despaired of redemption, and called upon God to have pity on us, and deliver us out of this obscurity, who also heard some of us, for when the cord came down the sixth time, some

Sexta.

hung themselves fast upon it, and whilst it swung from one side to the other, it came to me, which I suddenly catching, got uppermost, and so beyond all hope came out; whereat I exceedingly re-

Vulnus
exturro
Cæcitatis.

joyced, perceiving not the wound which in the drawing up I received on my head by a sharp stone, till I, with the rest of the released (as was always before done) was fain to help at the sev-

Septima.

enth and last pull, at which, through straining, the blood ran down my cloathes. This, nevertheless, through joy I regarded not.

When the last draught, whereon the most of all hung, was finished, the Matron caused the cord to be laid away, and willed

Magistræ
filius.

her aged son to declare her resolution to the rest of the prisoners, who thus spoke unto them.

> Ye children dear
>   All present here.
> What is but now compleat and done
> Was long before resolved on;
> Whate'er my mother of great grace
> To each on both sides here hath shown;
> May never discontent misplace!
> The joyful time is drawing on
> When every one shall equal be—
> None wealthy, none in penury.
> Whoe'er receiveth great commands
> Hath work enough to fill his hands

Whoe'er with much hath trusted been,
'Tis well if he may save his skin;
Wherefore, your lamentations cease,
What is't to waite for some few dayes?

The cover was now again put to and locked, the trumpets and kettle-drums began afresh, yet the bitter lamentation of the prisoners was heard above all, and soon caused my eyes to run over. Presently the Antient Matron, together with her son, sate down, and commanded the Redeemed should be told. As soon as she had written down their number in a gold-yellow tablet, she demanded everyone's name; this was also written down by a little page. Having viewed us all, she sighed, and said to her son—"Ah: how heartily am I grieved for the poor men in the dungeon! I would to God I durst release them all." Whereunto her son replied—"Mother, it is thus ordained by God, against Whom we may not contend. In case we all of us were lords, and were seated at table, who would there be to bring up the service!" At this his mother held her peace, but soon after she said—"Well, let these be freed form their fetters," which was presently done, and I, though among the last, could not refrain, but bowed myself before the Antient Matron, thanking God that through her had graciously vouchsafed to bring me out of darkness into light. The rest did likewise to the satisfaction of the matron. Lastly, to every one was given a piece of gold for a remembrance, and to spend by the way. On the one side thereof was stamped the rising sun; on the other these three letters D L S; therewith all had license to depart to his own business, with this intimation, *that we to the glory of God should benefit our neighbours, and reserve in silence what we had been intrusted with,* which we promised to do, and departed one from another. Because of the wounds the fetters had caused me, I could not well go forward, which the matron presently espying, calling me again to her side, said to me—"My son, let not this defect afflict thee, but call to mind thy infirmities, and thank God who hath permitted thee, even in this world, to come into so high a light. Keep these wounds for my sake."

Whereupon the trumpets began again to sound, which so affrighted me that I awoke, and perceived that it was onely a dream, which yet was so impressed on my imagination that I was perpetually troubled about it, and methought I was still sensible of the wounds on my feet. By all these things I well understood that God had vouchsafed me to be present at this mysterious and hidden Wedding, wherefore with childlike confidence I returned thanks to His Divine Majesty, and besought Him that He would preserve me in His fear, daily fill my heart with wisdom and understanding, and graciously conduct me to the desired end. Thereupon I prepared myself for the way, put on my white linnen coat, girded my loyns, with a blood-red ribbon bound cross-ways over my shoulder. In my hat I stuck four red roses, that I might the sooner by this token be taken notice of amongst the throng. For food I took bread, salt, and water, which by the counsel of an understanding person I had at certain times used, not without profit, in the like occurrences. Before I parted from my cottage, I first, in this my wedding garment, fell down upon my knees, and besought God to vouchsafe me a good issue. I made a vow that if anything should by His Grace be revealed to me, I would imploy it neither to my own honour nor authority in the world, but to the spreading of His name, and the service of my neighbour. With this vow I departed out of my cell with joy.

Magistra recens et evectos.

Secretarus.

Cur non omnes evecti.

Gratitudo auctoris evecti.

Nummus aureus.

☉

Deus Lux solis, vel Deo laus semper.

Mandatum Taciturnitatis.

Discessus autoris.

Vulnus ex compedibus.

Experget actio.

Solatium.

Precatio.

Præparatio ad iter.

Votum.

The Second Day.

I was hardly got out of my cell into a forrest when methought the whole heaven and all the elements had trimmed themselves against this wedding. Even the birds chanted more pleasantly than before, and the young fawns skipped so merrily that they rejoiced my old heart, and moved me also to sing with such a loud voice throughout the whole forrest, that it resounded from all parts, the hills repeating my last words, until at length I espyed a curious green heath, whither I betook myself out of the forrest. Upon this heath stood three tall cedars, which afforded an excellent shade, whereat I greatly rejoyced, for, although I had not gone far, my earnest longing made me faint. As soon as I came somewhat nigh, I espyed a tablet fastened to one of them, on which the following words were written in curious letters:—

God save thee, Stranger! If thou has heard anything concerning the nuptials of the King, consider these words. By us doth the Bridegroom offer thee a choice between foure ways, all of which, if thou dost not sink down in the way, can bring thee to his royal court. The first is short but dangerous, and one which will lead thee into rocky places, through which it will be scarcely possible to pass. The second is longer, and takes thee circuitously; it is plain and easy, if by the help of the Magnet, thou turnest neither to left nor right. The third is that truly royal way which through various pleasures and pageants of our King, affords thee a joyful journey; but this so far has scarcely been allotted to one in a thousand. By the fourth shall no man reach the place, because it is a consuming way, practicable onely for incorruptible bodys. Choose now which thou wilt of the three, and persevere constantly therein, for know whichsoever thou shalt enter, that is the one destined for thee by immutable Fate, nor const thou go back therein save at great peril to life. These are the things which we would have thee know, but, ho, beware! thou knowest not with how much danger thou dost commit thyself to this way, for if thou knowest thyself by the smallest fault to be obnoxious to the laws of our King, I beseech thee, while it is still possible, to return swiftly to thy house by the way which thou camest.

As soon as I had read this writing all my joy vanished, and I, who before sang merrily, began inwardly to lament. For although I saw all three ways before me, and it was vouchsafed me to make choice of one, yet it troubled me that in case I went the stony and rocky way, I might get a deadly fall; or, taking the long one, I might wander through byeways and be detained in the great journey. Neither durst I hope that I, amongst thousands, should be the one who should choose the Royal way. I saw likewise the fourth before me, but so invironed with fire and exhalation that I durst not draw near it, and, therefore, again and again considered whether I should turn back or take one of the ways before me. I well weighed my own unworthiness, and though the dream, that I was delivered out of the tower, still comforted me, yet I durst not confidently rely upon it. I was so perplexed that, nor great weariness, hunger and thirst seized me, whereupon I drew out my bread, cut a slice of it, which a snow-white dove, of whom I was not aware, sitting upon the tree, espyed and therewith came down, betaking herself very familiarly to me, to whom I willingly imparted my food, which she received, and with her prettiness did again a little refresh me. But as soon as her enemy, a most black Raven, perceived it, he straight darted down

Tripudium Creaturarum ob nuptias.

Per Sylvam.

In campam.

3 Cedri.
3 Templa.

Tabella mercurialis.
1.

☿

1.

2.

3.

4.

Via authoris eligenda.

Dubium.

Confirmatio.

Columba alba arbori mercuriali insidens.

Corvus niger.

upon the dove, and taking no notice of me, would needs force away her meat, who could not otherwise guard herself but by flight. Whereupon, both together flew toward the South, at which I was so hugely incensed and grieved, that without thinking, I made haste after the filthy Raven, and so, against my will, ran into one of the fore mentioned ways a whole fields length. The Raven being thus chased away, and the Dove delivered, I first observed what I had inconsiderately done, and that I was already entered into a way, from which, under peril of punishment, I durst not retire, and though I had still wherewith to comfort myself, yet that which was worst of all was, that I had left my bag and bread at the Tree, and could never retrieve them, for as soon as I turned myself about, a contrary wind was so strong against me that it was ready to fell me, but if I went forward, I perceived no hindrance, wherefore I patiently took up my cross, got upon my feet, and resolved I would use my utmost endeavour to get to my journey's end before night. Now, although many apparent byways showed themselves, I still proceeded with my compass, and would not budge one step from the meridian line. Howbeit, the way was oftentimes so rugged that I was in no little doubt of it. I constantly thought upon the Dove and Raven, and yet could not search out the meaning, until upon a high hill afar off I espyed a stately Portal, to which, not regarding that it was distant from the way I was in, I hasted, because the sun had already hid himself under the hills, and I could elsewhere see no abiding place, which I verily ascribe only to God, Who might have permitted me to go forward, and withheld my eyes that so I might have gazed beside this gate. to which I now made mighty haste, and reached it by so much daylight as to take a competent view of it. It was an exceeding Royal, beautiful Portal, whereon were carved a multitude of most noble figures and devices, every one of which (as I afterwards learned) had its peculiar signification. Above was fixed a pretty large Tablet, with these words, *"procul hinc procul ite profani,"* and more that I was forbidden to relate. As soon as I was come unto the portal, there streight stepped forth one in a sky-coloured habit, whom I saluted in friendly manner. Though he thankfully returned my greeting, he instantly demanded my Letter of Invitation. O how glad was I that I had brought it with me! How easily might I have forgotten it as chanced to others, as he himself told me. I quickly presented it, wherewith he was not only satisfied, but showed me abundance of respect, saying, "Come in, my Brother, an acceptable guest you are to me," withal entreating me not to withhold my name from him.

Versus Meridiem.

Autor in cidit in 2 viam incogitanter.

Compassus.

Diversorium. Occasus.

☉

Tabula inscriptionis.

Portitor.

Literæ convocationis.

Having replied that I was a Brother of the RED ROSIE CROSS, he both wondred and seemed to rejoyce at it, and then proceeded thus :—"My brother, have you nothing about you wherewith to purchase a token?" I answered my ability was small, but if he saw anything about me he had a mind to, it was at his service. Having requested of me my bottle of water, and I granting it, he gave me a golden token, whereon stood these letters, S.C., entreating me that when it stood me in good stead, I would remember him. After which I asked him how many were got in before me, which he also told me; and lastly, out of meer friendship, gave me a sealed letter to the second Porter. Having lingered some time with him the night grew on, whereupon a great beacon upon the gate was immediately fired, that if any were still upon the way, he might make haste thither. The road where it finished at the castle was enclosed with walls, and planted with all sorts

Nomen authoris.

Emitur aqua Tessera. Sanctitati constantia sponsus charus. Spes charitas. Diploma.

Castillum.

Virgo lucifera.

The Lady Chamberlain.

Porta secunda. Tabella. Custos Leo. 2 Portitor.

of excellent fruit trees. On every third tree on each side lanterns were hung up, wherein all the candles were lighted with a glorious torch by a beautiful Virgin, habited in skye colour, which was so noble and majestic a spectacle that I delayed longer then was requisite. At length, after an advantageous instruction, I departed from the first porter, and so went on the way, until I came to the second gate, which was adorned with images and mystick significations. In the affixed Tablet stood—*Date et dabitur vobis.* Under this gate lay a terrible Lyon, chained, who, as soon as he espied me, arose and made at me with great roaring, whereupon the second porter, who lay upon a stone of marble, awaked, and wishing me not to be troubled nor affrighted, drove back the lyon, and having received the letter, which I reached him with trembling hand, he read it, and with great respect spake thus to me :—"Now well-come in God's name unto me the man whom of long time I would gladly have seen!" Meanwhile, he also drew out a token, and asked me whether I could purchase it. But I, having nothing

Tessera empta sale. Studio merentis Sal humor Sponso mittendus Sal mineralis Sal menstrualis.

else left but my salt, presented it to him, which he thankfully accepted. Upon this token again stood two letters, namely, S.M. Being just about to discourse with him, it began to ring in the castle, whereupon the porter counselled me to run apace, or all the paines I had taken would serve to no purpose, for the lights above began already to be extinguished, whereupon I dispatched with much haste that I heeded not the porter; the virgin, after whom all the lights were put out, was at my heels, and I should never have found the way, had not she with her torch afforded me some light. I was more-over constrained to enter the very

Porta clauditur.

next to her, and the gates were so suddenly clapt to that a part of my coate was locked out, which I was forced to leave behind me, for neither I nor they who stood ready without and called at the gate could prevail with the porter to open it again. He delivered the keys to the virgin, who took them with her into the court. I again surveyed the gate, which now appeared so rich that the world could not equal it. Just by the door were two columns, on one of which stood a pleasant figure with this inscrip-

Pyramides portæ.

tion, *Congratulor.* On the other side was a statue with countenance veiled, and beneath was written, *Condoleo.* In brief, the inscriptions and figures thereon were so dark and mysterious that the most dexterous man could not have expounded them, yet all these I shall e'er long publish and explain. Under this gate I

Promissum authoris.

was again to give my name, which was written down in a little vellum-book, and immediately with the rest dispatched to the Lord Bridegroom. Here I first received the true guest-token, which was somewhat less than the former, but much heavier; upon this stood the letters S. P. N. Besides this, a new pair of

Salus per naturam sponsi præ sentandus nuptiis.

Comes puer.

shoes were given me, for the floor of the castle was pure shining marble. My old ones I was to give to one of the poor who sate in throngs under the gate. I bestowed them on an old man, after which two pages with as many torches conducted me into a little room, where they willed me to sit down upon a form, and, sticking their torches in two holes made in the pavement, they departed, and left me sitting alone. Soon after I heard a noise but saw nothing; it proved to be certain men who stumbled in upon me, but since I could see nothing I was fain to suffer and attend what

Balneatores.

they would do with me. Presently finding that they were barbers I intreated them not to jostle me, for I was content to do what they desired, whereupon one of them, whom I yet could not see,

Capillus detonsus

gently cut away the hair from the crown of my head, but on my forehead, ears, and eyes he permitted my icegrey locks to hang.

asservatus.

In this first encounter I was ready to despair, for, inasmuch as some of them shoved me so forceably, and were still invisible, I could onely think that God for my curiosity had suffered me to miscarry. The unseen barbers carefully gathered up the hair which was cut off, and carried it away. Then the two pages re-entered and heartily laughted at me for being so terrified. They had scarce spoken a few words with me when again a little bell began to ring, which (as the pages informed me) was to give notice for assembling, whereupon they willed me to rise, and through many walks, doors, and winding stairs lighted me into a spacious hall, where there was a great multitude of guests—emperors, kings, princes, and lords, noble and ignoble, rich and poor, and all sorts of people, at which I hugely marvelled, and thought to myself, "Ah! how gross a fool hast thou been to ingage upon this journey with so much bitterness and toil, when here are fellows whom thou well knowest, and yet hadst never any reason to esteem, while thou, with all thy prayers and supplications, art hardly got in at last."

Pueri bini.

Triclinium.

This and more the devil at that time injected. Meantime one or other of my acquaintance spake to me:—"Oh! Brother Rosencreutz, art thou here too?" "Yea, my brethren," I replied, "The grace of God hath helped me in also," at which they raised a mighty laughter, looking upon it as ridiculous that there should be need of God in so slight an occasion. Having demanded each of them concerning his way, and finding most of them were forced to clamber over rocks, certain invisible trumpets began to sound to the table, whereupon all seated themselves, every one as he judged himself above the rest, so that for me and some other sorry fellows there was hardly a little nook left at the lowermost table. Presently the two pages entred, and one of them said grace in so handsom and excellent a manner as rejoyced the very heart in my body. Howbeit, some made but little reckoning of them, but fleired and winked one at another, biting their lips within their hats, and using like unseemly gestures. After this, meat was brought in, and, albeit none could be seen, everything was so orderly managed that it seemed as if every guest had his proper attendant. Now my Artists having somewhat recruted themselves, and the wine having a little removed shame from their hearts, they presently began to vaunt of their abilities. One would prove this, another that, and commonly the most sorry idiots made the loudest noise. When I call to mind what preternatural and impossible enterprises I then heard, I am still ready to vomit at it. In fine, they never kept in their order, but whenever possible a rascal would insinuate himself among the nobles. Every man had his own prate, and yet the great lords were so simple that they believed their pretences, and the rogues became so audacious, that although some of them were rapped over th fingers with a knife, yet they flinched not at it, but when any one perchance had filched a gold-chain, then would all hazard for the like. I saw one who heard the movements of the Heavens, the second could see Plato's Ideas, a third could number the atoms of Democritus. There were not a few pretenders to perpetual motion. Many an one (in my opinion) had good understanding, but assumed too much to himself to his own destruction. Lastly, there was one who would needs persuade us that he saw the servitors who attended, and would have pursued his contention, had not one of those invisible waiters reached him so handsom a cuff upon his lying muzzle, that not only he, but many who were by him, became mute as mice. It best of all pleased me that those of whom I had any esteem were very quiet in their business, acknowledging themselves to be misunderstanding men for whom the mysteries

Impietas hostum non recta via ingressorum.

Quidam preces negligunt.

Commessatio.

Ministri invisibles.

Inebriatorum gloriatio vana.

Ministri invisibles.

Modestia proborum hospitum

of nature were too high. In this tumult I had almost cursed the day wherein I came hither, for I could not but with anguish behold that those lewd people were above at the board, but I in my sorry place could not even rest in quiet, one of these rascals scornfully reproaching me for a motley fool. I dreamed not that there was one gate behind through which we must pass, but imagined during the whole wedding I was to continue in this scorn and indignity which I had at no time deserved, either of the Lord Bride-groom or the Bride. And, therefore, I opined he would have done well to seek some other fool than me for his wedding. To such impatience doth the iniquity of this world reduce simple hearts. But this was really one part of the lameness whereof I had dreamed.

The longer all this clamour lasted, the more it increased. Howbeit, there sate by me a very fine, quiet man, who discoursed of excellent matters, and at length said:—"My Brother, if any one should come now who were willing to instruct these blockish people in the right way, would he be heard?" "No, verily," I replyed. "The world," said he, "is now resolved to be cheated, and will give no ear to those who intend its good. Seest thou that Cock's-comb, with what whimsical figures and foolish conceits he allures others. There one makes mouths at the people with unheard-of mysterious words. Yet the time is now coming when these shameful vizards shall be plucked off, and the world shall know what vagabond imposters were concealed behind them. Then perhaps that will be valued which at present is not esteemed."

While he was thus speaking, and the clamour was still increasing all on a sudden there began in the hall such excellent and stately musick of which, all the days of my life, I never heard the like. Every one held his peace, and attended what would come of it. There were all stringed instruments imaginable, sounding together in such harmony that I forgot myself, and sate so unmovably that those by me were amazed. This lasted nearly half an hour, wherein none of us spake one word, for as soon as anyone was about to open his mouth, he got an unexpected blow. After that space this musick ceased suddenly, and presently before the door of the hall began a great sounding and beating of trumpets, shalms, and kettle-drums, all so master-like as if the Emperor of Rome had been entring. The door opened of itself, and then the noise of the trumpets was so loud that we were hardly able to indure it. Meanwhile, many thousand small tapers came into the hall, marching of themselves in so exact an order as amazed us, till at last the two fore-mentioned pages with bright torches entred lighting in a most beautiful Virgin, drawn on a gloriously gilded, triumphant self-moving throne. She seemed to me the same who on the way kindled and put out the lights, and that these her attendants were the very ones whom she formerly placed at the trees. She was not now in skye-colour, but in a snow-white, glittering robe, which sparkled of pure gold, and cast such a lustre that we durst not steadily behold it. Both the pages were after the same manner habited, albeit somewhat more slightly. As soon as they were come into the middle of the hall, and were descended from the throne, all the small tapers made obeisance before her, whereupon we all stood up, and she having to us, as we again to her, shewed all respect and reverence, in a most pleasant tone she began thus to speak :—

"The King my Lord most gracious,
Who now's not very far from us,

[margin notes: Impatientia ex-iniquitate hominum. / Assessor modestus. / Mundus valt decipi. / Musica. / Mulctæ ab attendentium / Faculae ad lectum / Virgo lucifera. / The Lady Chamberlain / Albedo. / Salutatoria hospitum.]

As also his most lovely Bride,
To him in troth and honour tied,
Already, with great joy indued,
Have your arrival hither view'd;
And do to every one and all
Promise their grace in special;
And from their very heart's desire
You may the same in time acquire,
That so their future nuptial joy
May mixed be with none's annoy."

Hereupon, with all her small tapers, she again courteously bowed, and presently began thus:—

"In th' Invitation writ you know
That no man called was hereto
Who of God's rarest gifts good store
Had not received long before.
Although we cannot well conceit
That any man's so desperate,
Under conditions so hard,
Here to intrude without regard,
Unless he have been first of all
Prepared for this Nuptial,
And, therefore, in good hopes do dwell
That with all you it will be well;
Yet men are grown so bold and rude,
Not weighing their ineptitude,
As still to thrust themselves in place
Whereto none of them called was.
No cock's-comb here himself may sell,
No rascal in with others steal,
For we resolve without all let
A Wedding pure to celebrate.
So, then, the artists for to weigh,
Scales shall be fixt th' ensuing day;
Whereby each one may lightly find
What he hath left at home behind.
If here be any of that rout,
Who have good cause themselves to doubt,
Let him pack quickly hence aside,
Because in case he longer bide,
Of grace forelorn, and quite undone,
Betimes he must the gantlet run.
If any now his conscience gall,
He shall to-night be left in th' hall,
And be again release by morn,
Yet so he hither ne'er return.
If any man have confidence,
He with his waiter may go hence,
Who shall him to his chamber light,
Where he may rest in peace to-night."

Propositio actionis.

Probatio artificum

As soon as she had done speaking, she again made reverence, and sprung chearfully into her throne, after which the trumpets began again to sound, and conducted her invisibly away, but the most part of the small tapers remained, and still one of them accompanied each of us. In our perturbation, 'tis scarcely possible to express what pensive thoughts and gestures were amongst us, yet most part resolved to await the scale, and in case things sorted not well to depart (as they hoped) in peace. I had soon cast up

Autor humiliat se.

my reckoning, and seeing my conscience convinced me of all ignorance and unworthiness, I purposed to stay with the rest in the hall, and chose rather to content myself with the meal I had taken than to run the risk of a future repulse. After every one by his small taper had been severally conducted to a chamber (each, as I since understood, into a peculiar one), there staid nine of us, including he who discoursed with me at the table. Although our small tapers left us not, yet within an hour's time one of the pages came in, and, bringing a great bundle of cords with him, first demanded whether we had concluded to stay there, which when we had with sighs affirmed, he bound each of us in a several place, and so went away with our tapers, leaving us poor wretches in darkness. Then first began some to perceive the imminent danger, and myself could not refrain tears, for, although we were not forbidden to speak, anguish and affliction suffered none of us to utter one word. The cords were so wonderfully made that none could cut them, much less get them off his feet, yet this comforted me, that the future gain of many an one who had now betaken himself to rest would prove little to his satisfaction, but we by one night's pennance might expiate all our presumption. At

Somnium typicum.

What will be the issue of the probatory beam[He that climbs high hath a great fall.

length in my sorrowful thoughts I fell asleep, during which I had a dream which I esteem not impertinent to recount. Methought I was upon an high mountain, and saw before me a great valley, wherein were gathered an unspeakable multitude, each of whom had at his head a string by which he was hanging. Now one hung high, another low, some stood even quite upon the earth. In the air there flew up and down an ancient man, who had in his hand a pair of sheers, wherewith here he cut one's and there another's thread. Now he that was nigh the earth fell without noise, but when this happened to the high ones the earth quaked at their fall. To some it came to pass that their thread was so stretched they came to the earth before it was cut. I took pleasure at this tumbling, and it joyed me at the heart when he who had over-exalted himself in the air, of his wedding, got so shameful a fall that it carried even some of his neighbours along with him. In like manner it rejoyced me that he who had kept so near the earth could come down so gently that even his next men per-

Experget.

ceived it not. But in my highest fit of jollity, I was unawares jogged by one of my fellow-captives, upon which I waked and was much discontented with him. Howbeit, I considered my dream and recounted it to my brother, who lay by me on the other side, and who hoped some comfort might thereby be intended. In such discourse we spent the remaining part of the night, and with longing expected the day.

The Third Day.

As soon as the lovely day was broken, and the bright sun, having raised himself above the hills, had betaken himself to his appointed office, my good champions began to rise and leisurely make themselves ready unto the inquisition. Whereupon, one

Colloquium surgentium.

after another they came again into the hall, and giving us a good morrow, demanded how we had slept; and having espied our bonds some reproved us for being so cowardly, that we had not, as they, hazarded upon all adventures. Howbeit, some, whose hearts still smote them, made no loud cry of the business. We excused ourselves with our ignorance, hoping we should soon be set at liberty and learn wit by this disgrace, that they also had not altogether escaped, and perhaps their greatest danger was still to be ex-

Cantus.

pected. At length all being assumbled, the trumpets began again to sound and the kettle-drums to beat, and we imagined that the Bride-groom was ready to present himself, which, nevertheless, was a huge mistake, for again it was the Virgin, who had arrayed herself all in red velvet, and girded herself with a white scarfe. Upon her head she had a green wreath of laurel, which much became her. Her train was no more of small tapers, but consisted of two hundred men in harness all cloathed, like herself, in red and white. As soon as they were alighted from the throne, she comes streight to us prisoners, and, after she had saluted us, said in few words:—"That some of you have been sensible of your wretched condition is pleasing to my most mighty Lord, and he is also resolved you shall fare the better for it." Having espied me in my habit, she laughed and spake:—"Good lack! Hast thou also submitted thyself to the yoke! I imagined thou wouldst have made thyself very snug," which words caused my eyes to run over. After this she commanded we should be unbound, cuppled together, and placed in a station where we might well behold the scales. "For," she said, "it may fare better with them than with the presumptuous who yet stand at liberty."

Virgo lucifera. The Lady Chamberlain.

Solatur humiles.

Meantime the scales, which were intirely of gold, were hung up in the midst of the hall. There was also a little table covered with red velvet, and seven weights thereon—first of all stood a pretty great one, then four little ones, lastly, two great ones severally, and these weights in proportion to their bulk were so heavy that no man can believe or comprehend it. Each of the harnised men carried a naked sword and a strong rope. They were distributed according to the number of weights into seven bands, and out of every band was one chosen for their proper weight, after which the Virgin again sprung up into her high throne, and one of the pages commanded each to place himself according to his order, and successively step into the scale. One of the Emperors, making no scruple, first bowed himself a little towards the Virgin, and in all his stately attire went up, whereupon each captain laid in his weight, which (to the wonder of all) he stood out. But the last was too heavy for him, so that forth he must, and that with such anguish that the Virgin herself seemed to pitty him, yet was the good Emperor bound and delivered to the sixth band. Next him came forth another Emperor, who stept hautily into the scale, and, having a thick book under his gown, he imagined not to fail; but, being scarce able to abide the third weight, he was unmercifully slung down, and his book in that affrightment slipping from him, all the soldiers began to laugh, and he was delivered up bound to the third band. Thus it went also with some others of the Emperors, who were all shamefully laughed at and made captive. After these comes forth a little short man, with a curled brown beard, an Emperor too, who, after the usual reverence, got up and held out so stedfastly that methought had there been more weights he would have outstood them. To him the Virgin immediately arose and bowed before him, causing him to put on a gown of red velvet, then reaching him a branch of laurel, whereof she had good store upon her throne, on the steps of which she willed him to sit down. How after him it fared with the rest of the Emperors, Kings, and Lords, would be too long to recount; few of those great personages held out, though sundry eminent vertues were found in many. Everyone who failed was miserably laughed at by the bands. After the inquisition had passed over the gentry, the learned, and unlearned, in each condition one, it may be, two, but mostly none, being found perfect, it came to those vagabond cheaters and rascally *Lapidem Spitalanficum* makers, who were set upon the scale with such

Libra aurea.

7. Pondera.

Satellites.

Pendesantur artifices.
1. Cæsar.

2. Cæsar.

3. Alii Cæsares.
4. Cæsar.

Proba falsariorum.

scorn, that for all my grief I was ready to burst my belly with laughing, neither could the prisoners themselves refrain, for the most part could not abide that severe trial, but with whips and scourges were jerked out of the scale. Thus of so pert a throng so few remained that I am ashamed to discover their number. Howbeit, there were persons of quality also amongst them who, notwithstanding, were also honoured with velvet robes and wreaths of laurel.

Nobiles nihilominus ornantur.

The inquisition being finished, and none but we poor coupled hounds standing aside, one of the captains stept forth, and said:— "Gratious madam, if it please your ladyship, let these poor men, who acknowledge their misunderstanding, be set upon the scale also without danger of penalty, and only for recreation's sake, if perchance anything right be found among them." At this I was in great perplexity, for in my anguish this was my only comfort, that I was not to stand in such ignominy, or be lashed out of the scale. Yet since the Virgin consented, so it must be, and we being untied were one after another set up. Now, although the most part miscarried, they were neither laughed at nor scourged, but peaceably placed on one side. My companion was the fifth, who held out bravely, whereupon all, but especially the captain who made the request for us, applauded him, and the Virgin showed him the usual respect. After him two more were despatched in an instant. But I was the eighth, and as soon as (with trembling) I stepped up, my companion, who already sat by in his velvet, looked friendly upon me, and the Virgin herself smiled a little. But, for as much as I outstayed all the weights, the Virgin commanded them to draw me up by force, wherefore three men moreover hung on the otherside of the beam, and yet could nothing prevail. Whereupon one of the pages immediately stood up, and cryed out exceeding loud, "THAT IS HE," upon which the other replyed:—"Then let him gain his liberty!" which the Virgin accorded, and being received with due ceremonies, the choice was given me to release one of the captives, whosoever I pleased, whereupon I made no long deliberations, but elected the first Emperor, whom I had long pitied, who was immediately set free, and with all respect seated among us. Now, the last being set up the weights proved too heavy for him; meanwhile the Virgin espied my roses, which I had taken out of my hat into my hands, and thereupon by her page graciously requested them of me, which I readily sent her. And so this first act was finished about ten in the forenoon.

Proba Humilium.

Socius Autoris.

Autor.

That is he.

Probatissimus.

Liberat, 1. Cæsarem.

Autor rosam suam donat virgini. Hora, 10. Actus.

The trumpets again began to sound, which, nevertheless, we could not as yet see. Meantime the bands were to step aside with their prisoners and expect the judgment, after which a council should be stripped and caused to run out naked, while others yet of the seven captains and ourselves was set, with the Virgin as president, whereat it was concluded that all the principal lords should with befitting respect be led out of the castle, that others should be stripped and caused to run out naked, while others yet with rods, whips, or dogs, should be hunted out. Those who the day before willingly surrendered themselves might be suffered to depart without any blame, but those presumptuous ones, and they who had behaved themselves so unseemly at dinner, should be punished in body and life according to each man's demerit. This opinion pleased the Virgin well, and obtained the upper hand. There was moreover another dinner vouchsafed them, the execution itself being deferred till noon. Herewith the senate arose, and the Virgin, together with her attendants, returned to her usual quarter. The uppermost table in the room was allotted to

Judicium de reprobatis.

us till the business was fully dispatched, when we should be conducted to the Lord Bride-groom and Bride, with which we were well content. The prisoners were again brought into the hall, and each man seated according to his quality. They were enjoyned to behave somewhat more civilly than they had done the day before, which admonishment they needed not, for they had already put up their pipes, and this I can boldly say, that commonly those who were of highest rank best understood how to comport themselves in so unexpected a misfortune. Their treatment was but indifferent, yet with respect, neither could they see their attendants, who were visible to us, whereat I was exceeding joyful. Although fortune had exalted us, we took not upon us more than the rest, advising them to be of good cheer, and comforting them as well as we could, drinking with them to try if the wine might make them cheerful. Our table was covered with red velvet, beset with drinking cups of pure silver and gold, which the rest could not behold without amazement and anguish. Ere we had seated ourselves in came the two pages, presenting every one, in the Bride-groom's behalf, the Golden Fleece with a flying Lyon, requesting us to wear them at the table, and to observe the reputation and dignity of the order which his Majesty had vouchsafed us and would ratify with sutable ceremonies. This we received with profoundest submission, promising to perform whatever his Majesty should please. Beside these, the noble page had a schedule wherein we were set down in order. Now because our entertainment was exceeding stately, we demanded one of the pages whether we might have leave to send some choice bit to our friends and acquaintance, who making no difficulty, every one sent by the waiters; howbeit the receivers saw none of them; and forasmuch as they knew not whence it came, I was myself desirous to carry somewhat to one of them, but, as soon as I was risen, one of the waiters was at my elbow, desiring me to take friendly warning, for in case one of the pages had seen it, it would have come to the King's ear, who would certainly take it amiss of me; but since none had observed it save himself, he purposed not to betray me, and that I must for the time to come have better regard to the dignity of the order. With these words, the servant did really so astonish me that for long I scarce moved upon my seat, yet I returned him thanks for his faithful warning as well as I was able. Soon after the drums began to beat, wherefore we prepared ourselves to recive the Virgin, who now came in the King's behalf, saying that it was brought from his Majesty, before her a very tall goblet of gold, and the other a patent in parchment. Being now after a marvellous articial manner alighted from her seat, she takes the goblet from the page and presents it in the King's behalf, saying that it was brought from his Majesty, and that in honour of him we should cause it to go round. Upon the cover of this goblet stood Fortune curiously cast in gold, who had in her hand a red flying ensign, for which cause I drunk somewhat the more sadly, as having been too well acquainted with Fortune's waywardness. But the Virgin who also was adorned with the Golden Fleece and Lyon, hereupon began to distinguish the patent which the other page held into two different parts, out of which thus much was read before the first company :—

That they should confess that they had too lightly given credit to false, fictitious books, had assumed too much to themselves, and so come into this castle uninvited, and perhaps designing to make their markets here and afterwards to live in the greater pride and lordliness. Thus one had seduced another, and plunged him into disgrace and ignominy, wherefore they were

Prandium.

Ministri invisibles visibles.

Proborum exaltatio.

Remuneratio a sponso.

Autori denegatur communicatio erga reprobos.

Virgo lucifera. The Lady Chamberlain.

Calix obambulans.

Ornatus virginis.

Reprobi dividuntur.

Accusatio unius partis.

Affectibus mundanis.

deservedly to be soundly punished—all which they, with great humility, readily acknowledged, and gave their hands upon it, after which a severe check was given to the rest, much to this purpose :—

Alterius partis.

That they were convinced in their consciences of forging false. fictitious books, had befooled and cheated others, thereby diminishing regal dignity amongst all. They knew what ungodly, deceitful figures they had made use of, not even sparing the Divine Trinity. It was also clear as day with what practices they had endeavoured to ensnare the guests ; in like manner, it was manifest to all the world that they wallowed in open whoredom, adultery, gluttony. and other uncleannesses. In brief, they had disparaged Kingly Majesty, even amongst the common sort, and therefore should confess themselves to be convicted vagabond-cheats, and rascals, for which they deserved to be cashiered from the company of civil people, and severely to be punished.

Excusatio.

The good Artists were loath to come to this confession, but inasmuch as the Virgin not only herself threatned, and sware their death, but the other party also vehemently raged at them, crying that they had most wickedly seduced them out of the Light, they at length, to prevent a huge misfortune, confessed the same with dolour, yet alledged their actions should not be animadverted upon in the worst sense, for the Lords were resolved to get into the castle, and had promised great sums of money to that effect, each one had used all craft to seize upon something, and so things were brought to the present pass. Thus they had disserved no more than the Lords themselves. Their books also sold so mightily that whoever had no other means to maintain himself was fain to ingage in this consonage. They hoped, moreover, they should be found no way to have miscarried, as having behaved towards the Lords, as became servants, upon their earnest entreaty. But

Refutatio.

answer was made that his Royal Majesty had determined to punish all, albeit one more severely than another. For although what they had alledged was partly true, and therefore the Lords should not wholly be indulged, yet they had good reason to prepare themselves for death, who had so presumptuously obtruded themselves, and perhaps seduced the ignorant against their will.

Dolor de sententia.

Thereupon many began most pitteously to lament and prostrate themselves, all which could avail them nothing, and I much marvelled how the Virgin could be so resolute, when their misery caused our eyes to run over. She presently dispatched her page, who brought with him all the cuirassiers which had been appointed at the scales, who were each commanded to take his own man, and, in an orderly procession, conduct him into her great garden.

Executio sententiarum.

Leave was given to my yesterday companions to go out into the garden unbound, and be present at the execution of the sentence.

Spectatores.

When every man was come forth, the Virgin mounted up into her high throne, requesting us to sit down upon the steps, and appear at the judgment. The goblet was committed to the pages' keeping, and we went forth in our robes upon the throne, which of itself moved so gently as if we had passed in the air, till we came into the garden, where we arose altogether.

Hortus.

This garden was not extraordinarily curious, only it pleased me that the trees were planted in so good order. Besides there ran in it a most costly fountain, adorned with wonderful figures and inscriptions and strange characters (which, God willing, I shall mention in a future book).

Autor promittit alter librum.

In this garden was raised a wooden scaffold, hung with curiously painted figured coverlets. There were four galleries made one over another; the first was more glorious than the rest and covered with a white Taffata curtain, so that we could not perceive who was behind it. The second was empty and uncovered, while the two last were draped with red and blew Taffeta. As soon as we were come to the scaffold the Virgin bowed herself down to the ground, at which we were mightily terrified, for we could easily guess that the King and Queen must not be far off. We also having duely performed our reverence, the Virgin led us by the winding stairs into the second gallery, where she placed herself uppermost, and us in our former order. But how the emperor whom I had released behaved towards me, I cannot relate for fear of slander, for he might well imagine in what anguish he now should have been, and that only through me he had attained such dignity and worthiness. Meantime, the virgin who first brought me the invitation, and whom I had hitherto never since seen, stepped in, and giving one blast upon her trumpet declared the sentence with a very loud voice :—

Gratitudo Cæsaris erga liberatorem.

"The King's Majesty, my most gratious Lord, could from his heart wish that all here assembled had, upon his Majestie's invitation, presented themselves so qualified that they might have adorned his nuptial and joyous Feast. But since it hath otherwise pleased Almighty God, he hath not wherewith to murmur, but is forced, contrary to his inclination, to abide by the ancient and laudable constitutions of this Kingdom, albeit, that his Majesty's clemency may be celebrated, the usual sentence shall be considerably lenified. He vouchsafes to the Lords and Potentates not only their lives intirely, but also freely dismisses them, courteously intreating your Lordships not to take it in evil part that you cannot be present at his Feast of Honour. Neither is your reputation hereby prejudiced, although you be rejected by this our Order, since we cannot at once do all things, and forasmuch as your Lordships have been seduced by base rascals, it shall not pass unrevenged. Furthermore, his Majesty resolveth shortly to communicate with you a Catalogue of Hereticks, or Index Expurgatorius, that you may with better judgment discern between good and evil. And because his Majesty also purposeth to rummage his library, and offer the seductive writings to Vulcan, he courteously entreats every one of you to put the same in execution with your own, whereby it is to be hoped that all evil and mischief may be remedied. And you are admonished never henceforth so inconsiderately to covet entrance hither, least the former excuse of seducers be taken from you. In fine, as the estates of the Land have still somewhat to demand of your Lordships, his Majesty hopes that no man will think it much to redeem himself with a chain, or what else he hath about him, and so, in friendly manner, depart from us.

Oratio ad judicados.

Sententia magnatum.

"The others who stood not at the first, third, and fourth weight, his Majesty will not so lightly dismiss, but that they also may experience his gentleness, it is his command to strip them naked, and so send them forth. Those who in the second and fifth weight were found too light shall, besides stripping, be noted with one or more brands, according to each was lighter or heavier. They who were drawn up by the sixth or seventh shall be somewhat more gratiously dealt with, and so forward, for unto every combination there is a certain punishment ordained. They who yesterday separated themselves of their own accord shall go at liberty without blame. Finally, the convicted vagabond-cheats, who could move up none of the weights, shall be punished, in body and life, with sword, halter, water, and rods, and such execution of judgment shall be inviolably observed for an example unto others."

Sententia, 2.

3.

4.

5.
6.

Finis habiti
judici.

Reorum
mores.

Ministrorum
mores.

Haustus
oblivionis.

Damnati.

Commise-
rationis
expositio.
Unicorna.

Leo.

Machæra.

Columba.

Discessus
ab hoc actu.

Discessus
virgini
luciferæ.

Hospitum
modi in
delecta-
mentis.

Autoris.

Herewith one virgin broke her wand; the other, who read the sentence, blew her trumpet, and stepped with profound reverence towards the curtain. Now this judgment being read over, the Lords were well satised, for which cause they gave more than they were desired, each one redeeming himself with chains, jewels, gold, monies, and other things, and with reverence they took leave. Although the King's servants were forbidden to jear any at his departure, some unlucky birds could not hold laughing, and certainly it was sufficiently ridiculous to see them pack away with such speed, without once looking behind them. At the door was given to each of them a draught of FORGETFULNESS, that he might have no further memory of misfortune. After these the volunteers departed, who, because of their ingenuity, were suffered to pass, but so as never to return in the same fashion, albeit if to them (as likewise to the others) anything further were revealed, they should be well-come guests.

Meanwhile, others were stripping, in which also an inequality, according to demerit, was observed. Some were sent away naked, without other hurt; others were driven out with small bells; some again were scourged forth. In brief, the punishments were so various, that I am not able to recount them all. With the last a somewhat longer time was spent, for whilst some were hanging, some beheading, some forced to leap into the water, much time was consumed. Verily, at this execution my eyes ran over, not indeed in regard to the punishment which impudency well deserved, but in contemplation of human blindness, in that we are continually busying ourselves over that which since the first fall hath been sealed to us. Thus the garden which lately was quite full was soon emptied. As soon as this was done, and silence had been kept for the space of five minutes, there came forward a beautiful snow-white Unicorn, with a golden collar, ingraved with certain letters, about his neck. He bound himself down upon his fore-feet, as if hereby he had shown honour to the Lyon, who stood so immoveably upon the fountain that I took him to be stone or brass, but who immediately took the naked sword which he bare in his paw, brake it into two in the middle, the two pieces whereof sunk into the fountain, after which he so long reared until a white Dove brought a branch of olive in her bill, which the Lyon devoured in an instant, and so was quieted. The Unicorn returned to his place with joy, while our Virgin led us down by the winding staires from the scaffold, and so we again made our reverence towards the curtain. We washed our hands and heads in the fountain, and thereby waited in order till the King through a secret gallery returned into his hall, and then we also, with choice musick, pomp, state, and pleasant discourse, were conducted into our former lodging. Here, that the time might not seem too long to us, the Virgin bestowed on each of us a noble Page, not only richly habited but also exceeding learned, and able aptly to discourse on all subjects, so that we had reason to be ashamed of ourselves. These were commanded to lead us up and down the castle, yet only in certain places, and, if possible, to shorten the time according to our desire. Meantime, the Virgin took leave, promising to be with us again at supper, and after that to celebrate the ceremonies of hanging up the weights, while on the morrow we should be presented to the King. Each of us now did what best pleased him, one part viewing the excellent paintings, which they copied for themselves, and considered what the wonderful characters might signify, others recruiting themselves with meat and drink. I caused my Page to conduct me, with my Companion, up and down the castle, of which walk it will never repent me so long as I live.

Besides many other glorious antiquities, the Royal Sepulcher was shewed me, by which I learned more than is extant in all books. There in the same place stands the glorious Phœnix, of which two years since I published a small discourse, and am resolved, in case this narrative prove useful, to set forth several treatises concerning the Lyon, Eagle, Griffon, Falcon, &c., together with their draughts and inscriptions. It grieves me also for my other consorts that they neglected such pretious treasures. I indeed reaped the most benefit by my Page, for according as each one's genius lay, so he led his intrusted one into the quarters pleasing to him. Now the kyes hereunto belonging were committed to my Page, and, therefore, this good fortune happened to me before the rest, for though he invited others to come in, yet they imagining such tombs to be only in the churchyard, thought they should well enough get thither whenever anything was to be seen there. Neither shall these monuments be with-held from my thankful schollars. The other thing that was shewed us two was the noble Library as it was altogether before the Reformation, of which I have so much the less to say, because the catalogue is shortly to be published. At the entry of this room stands a great Book the like whereof I never saw, in which all the figures, rooms, portals, writings, riddles, and the like, to be seen in the whole castle are delineated. In every book stands its author painted, whereof many were to be burnt, that even their memory might be blotted out from amongst the righteous. Having taken a full view, and being scarce gotten forth, there comes another Page, and having whispered somewhat in our Page's ear, he delivered up the kyes to him, who immediately carried them up the winding stairs; but our Page was very much out of countenance, and we, setting hard upon him with intreaties, he declared to us that the King's Majesty would by no means permit that either the library or sepulchers should be seen by man, and he besought us as we tendered his life to dicover it not to anyone, he having already utterly denyed it; whereupon both of us stood hovering between joy and fear, yet it continued in silence, and no man made further inquiry about it. Thus in both places we consumed three hours, and now, although it had struck seven, nothing was hitherto given us to eat, but our hunger was abated by constant revivings, and I could be content to fast all my life with such an entertainment. About this time the curious fountains, mines, and all kind of art shops were also shown us, of which there was none but surpassed all our arts even if melted into one mass. Every chamber was built in semi-circle, that so they might have before their eyes the costly clock-work which was erected upon a fair turret in the centre, and regulate themselves according to the course of the planets which were to be seen on it in a glorious manner. At length I came into a spacious room, in the middle whereof stood a terrestrial globe, whose diameter contained thirty foot, albeit near half, except a little which was covered with the steps, was let into the earth. Two men might readily turn it about, so that more of it was never to be seen but so much as was above the horizon. I could not understand whereto those ringlets of gold (which were upon it in several places) served, at which my Page laughed, and advised me to view them more narrowly, when I found there my native country noted with gold also, whereupon my companion sought his and found that too. The same happened to others who stood by, and the Page told us that it was yesterday declared to the King's Majesty by their old astronomer Atlas, that all the gilded points did exactly answer to their native countries, and, therefore, he, as soon as he perceived that I undervalued

Libellus de Phœnice.

Usus eorum quæ autor vidit.

Bibliotheca.

Fastidium pulsum egregiis spectaculis.

Officinarum constitutarum finis.

Globus terrenus.

myself, but that nevertheless there stood a point upon my native country, moved one of the captains to intreat for us to be set upon the scale at all adventures, especially seeing one of our native countries had a notable good mark. And truly it was not without cause that he, the Page of greatest power, was bestowed on me. For this I returned him thanks, and looking more diligently upon my native country, I found that, besides the ringlets, there were also certain delicate streaks upon it. I saw much more even upon this globe than I am willing to discover. Let each man take into consideration why every city produceth not a philosopher. After this he led us within the globe, for on the sea there was a tablet (whereon stood three dedications and the author's name) which a man might gently lift up, and by a little board go into the center, which was capable of four persons, being nothing but a round board whereon we could sit and at ease by broad daylight (it was now already dark) contemplate the stars, which seemed like mere carbuncles glittering in an agreeable order, and moving so gallantly that I had scarce any mind ever to go out again, as the Page afterwards told the Virgin, and with which she often twitted me, for it was already supper time and I was almost the last at table. The waiters treated me with so much reverence and honour that for shame I durst not look up. To speak concerning the musick, or the rest of that magnificent entertainment, I hold needless, because it is not possible sufficiently to express it. In brief there was nothing there but art and amenity. After we had each to other related our employment since noon (howbeit, not a word was spoken of the library and monuments), being already merry with wine, the Virgin began thus:—"My Lords, I have a great contention with one of my sisters. In our chamber we have an eagle, whom we cherish with such diligence that each of us is desirous to be the best beloved, and upon that score have many a squabble. On a day we concluded to go both together to him, and toward whom he should show himself most friendly, hers should he properly be. This we did, and I, as commonly, bare in my hand a branch of lawrel, but my sister had none. As soon as he espyed us both, he gave my sister another branch which he had in his beak, and offered at mine, which I gave him. Each of us hereupon imagined herself best beloved of him. Which way am I to resolve myself?"

This modest proposal pleased us mightily well, and each one would gladly have heard the solution, but inasmuch as all looked upon me, and desired to have the beginning from me, my mind was so extreamly confounded that I knew not what to do but propound another in its stead, and said, therefore:—"Gracious Lady, your Ladyship's question were easily to be resolved if one thing did not perplex me. I had two companions who both loved me exceedingly; they being doubtful which was most dear to me, concluded to run to me unawares, and that he whom I should then embrace should be the right; this they did, yet one of them could not keep pace with the other, so he staid behind and wept; the other I embraced with amazement. When they had afterwards discovered the business to me, I knew not how to resolve, and have hitherto let it rest in this manner till I may find some good advice herein."

The Virgin wondered at it, and well observed where about I was, upon which she replied, that we should both be quit, and then desired the solution from the rest. But I had already made them wise, wherefore the next began thus—"In my city a Virgin was condemned to death, but the judge being pittiful towards her,

Excellentia patriæ autoris.

Quid in glob.

Reverentia in convivio exhibita auctoris.

The Lady Chamberlain.

Perplexed speeches, or intricate questions.

Autoris griphus.

The Author's counter-demand.

Griphus, 2.

proclaimed that if any man desired to be her champion, he should
have free leave. Now she had two lovers; one made himself
ready, and came into the lists to expect his adversary; afterwards
the other presented himself, but coming too late, resolved nevertheless to fight, and suffer himself to be vanquished that the
Virgin's life might be preserved, which succeeded accordingly.
Thereupon each challenged her, and now, my lords, instruct me to
which of them of right she belongeth." The Virgin could hold no
longer, but said:—"I thought to have gained much information,
and am my self gotten into the net; yet I would gladly hear
whether there be any more behind." "Yes, that there is," answered the third, "a stranger adventure hath not been recounted
then that which happened to myself. In my youth I loved a
worthy maid, and that my love might attain its end I made use
of an ancient matron, who easily brought me to her. Now it
happened that the maid's brethren came in upon us as we three
were together, and were in such a rage that they would have taken
my life, but, on my vehement supplication, they at length forced
me to swear to take each of them for a year to my wedded wife.
Now, tell me, my Lords, should I take the old or the young one
first?" We all laughed sufficiently at this riddle, yet none would
undertake to unfold it, and the fourth began. "In a certain city
there dwelt an honourable lady, beloved of all, but especially of a
noble young man, who would needs be too importunate with her.
At length she gave him this determination, that in case he would,
in a cold winter, lead her into a fair green garden of Roses, then
he should obtain, but if not he must resolve never to see her more.
The noble man travelled into all countries to find one who might
perform this, till at length he lite upon a little old man who
promised to do it for him, in case he would assure him of half
his estate, which he having consented to the other was as good as
his word. Whereupon he invited the Lady home to his garden,
where, contrary to her expectation, she found all things green,
pleasant, and warm; and remembering her promise, she only requested that she might once more return to her lord, to whom
with sighs and tears she bewailed her lamentable condition. Her
lord, sufficiently perceiving her faithfulness, dispatched her back
to her lover, who had so dearly purchased her, that she might give
him satisfaction, when the husband's integrity so mightily affected
the noble man that he thought it a sin to touch so honest a wife,
and sent her home with honour to her lord. The little man, perceiving such faith in all these, would not, how poor soever he
were, be the least, but restored the noble man all his goods, and
went his way. Now, my lords, which of these persons showed
the greatest ingenuity?" Here our tongues were quite cut off,
neither would the Virgin make any reply but that another should
go on; wherefore the fifth began:—"I desire not to make long
work. Who hath the greater joy, he that beholdeth what he
loveth, or he that only thinketh on it?" "He that beholdeth it,"
said the Virgin. "Nay," answered I, and hereupon rose a contest
till the sixth called out:—"My lords, I am to take a wife; I have
before me a maid, a married wife, and a widdow; ease me of this
doubt, and I will help to order the rest." "It goes well there,"
replied the seventh, "when a man hath his choice, but with me
the case is otherwise. In my youth I loved a fair and virtuous
virgin, and she me in like manner; howbeit, because of her friends'
denyal, we could not come together in wedlock, whereupon she
was married to another, who maintained her honourably and with
affection, till she came into the pains of childbirth, which went so
hard with her that all thought she was dead, so with much state
and mourning she was interred. Now, I thought with myself,

Griphus, 4.

Griphus, 5.

Griphus, 6.

7.

8.

during her life thou couldst have no part in this woman, but dead as she is, thou mayst embrace her sufficiently, whereupon I took my servant with me, who dug her up by night. Having opened the coffin and locked her in my arms, I found some little motion in her heart, which increased from my warmth, till I perceived she was indeed alive. I quietly bore her home, and after I had warmed her chilled body with a costly bath of herbs, I committed her to my mother until she brought forth a fair son, whom I caused faithfully to be nursed. After two days (she being then in a mighty amazement) I discovered to her all the affair, requesting that for the time to come she would live with me as a wife, against which she excepted thus, in case it should be grievous to her husband, who had maintained her well and honourably, but if it could otherwise be, she was the present obliged in love to one as well as the other. After two months (being then to make a journey elsewhere) I invited her husband as a guest, and amongst other things demanded of him whether if his deceased wife should come home again he could be content to receive her, and he affirming it with tears and lamentations, I brought him his wife and son, recounting all the fore-passed business, and intreating him to ratifie with his consent my fore-purposed espousals. After a long dispute he could not beat me from my right, but was fain to leave me the wife. But still the contest was about the son." Here the Virgin interrupted him and said:—"It makes me wonder how you could double the afflicted man's grief." Upon this there arose a dispute amongst us, the most part affirming he had done but right. "Nay," said he, "I freely returned him both his wife and son. Now tell me, my lords, was my honesty or this man's joy the greater?" These words so mightily cheared the Virgin that she caused a health to go round, after which other proposals went on somewhat perplexedly, so that I could not retain them all; yet this comes to my mind, that one told how a few years before he had

9.

seen a physitian who bought a parcel of wood against winter, with which he warmed himself all winter long; but as soon as spring returned he sold the very same wood again, and so had the use of it for nothing. "Here must needs be skill," said the Virgin, "but the time is now past." "Yea," replyed my companion, "whoever understands how to resolve all the riddles may give notice of it by a proper messenger; I conceive he will not be denied." At this time they began to say grace, and we arose altogether from the table rather satisfied and merry than glutted; it were to be wished that all invitations and feastings were thus kept. Having taken some few turns up and down the hall, the Virgin asked

Virgo
lucifera
gratiositas.

us whether we desired to begin the wedding. "Yes," said one, "noble and vertuous lady;" whereupon she privately dispatched a Page, and, meantime, proceeded in discourse with us. In brief, she was become so familiar that I adventured and requested her Name. The Virgin smiled at my curiosity, and replyed:—"My

Ænigma
de Nomine.

name contains five and fifty, and yet hath only eight letters; the third is the third part of the fifth, which added to the sixth will produce a number, whose root shall exceed the third itself by just the first, and it is the half of the fourth. Now the fifth and seventh are equal, the last and first also equal, and make with the second as much as the sixth hath, which contains four more than the third tripled. Now tell me, my lord, how am I called?"

The answer was intricate enough, yet I left not off, but said:— "Noble and vertuous Lady, may I not obtain one only letter?" "Yea," said she, "that may well be done." "What, then," I pro-

60, Sc. quot
virgines.

ceeded, "may the seventh contain?" "It contains," said she, "as many as there are lords here." With this I easily found her Name, at which she was well pleased, saying that much more should yet be revealed to us. Meantime certain virgins had made themselves ready, and came in with great ceremony. Two youths carried lights before them, one of whom was of jocond countenance, sprightly eyes, and gentile proportion, while the other lookt something angerly, and whatever he would have must be, as I afterwards perceived. Four Virgins followed them ; one looked shamefully towards the earth ; the second also was a modest, bashful Virgin ; the third, as she entered, seemed amazed at somewhat, and, as I understood, she cannot well abide where there is too much mirth. The fourth brought with her certain small wreaths, to manifest her kindness and liberality. After these four came two somewhat more gloriously apparelled ; they saluted us courteously. One of them had a gown of skeye-colour, spangled with golden stars : the other's was green, beautified with red and white stripes. On their heads they had thin flying white tiffaties, which did most becomingly adorn them. At last came one alone, wearing a coronet, and rather looking up towards heaven than towards earth. We all took her for the Bride, but were much mistaken, although in honour, riches, and state she much surpassed the bride, and afterwards ruled the whole Wedding. On this occasion we all followed our Virgin, and fell on our knees ; howbeit, she shewed herself extreamly humble, offering each her hand, and admonishing us not to be too much surprized at this, which was one of her smallest bounties, but to lift up our eyes to our Creator and acknowledge his Omnipotency, and so proceed in our enterprised course, employing this grace to the praise of God and the good of man. In sum her words were quite different from those of our Virgin, who was somewhat more worldly. They pierced even through my bones and marrow. "Thou," said she further to me, "hast received more than others ; see that thou also make a larger return."

This to me was a very strange sermon, for as soon as we saw the Virgins with the musick, we imagined we should fall to dancing. Now the Weights stood still in the same place, wherefore the Queen (I yet know not who she was) commanded each Virgin to take up one, but to our Virgin she gave her own, which was the largest, and commanded us to follow behind. Our majesty was then somewhat abated, for I observed that our Virgin was but too good for us, and that we were not so highly reputed as we ourselves were almost willing to phantsie. We were brought into the first Chamber, where our Virgin hung up the Queen's weight, during which an excellent spiritual hymn was sung. There was nothing costly in this room save certain curious little Prayer-Books which should never be missing. In the midst was a pulpit, convenient for prayer, where in the Queen kneeled down, and about her we also were fain to kneel and pray after the Virgin, who read out of a book, that this Wedding might tend to the honour of God, and our own benefit. We then came into the second chamber, where the first Virgin hung up her weight also, and so forward till all the ceremonies were finished, upon which the Queen again presented her hand to every one, and departed with her Virgins. Our president staied awhile with us, but because it had been already two hours night she would then no longer detain us, and, though methought she was glad of our company, she bid us good night, wishing us quiet rest. Our Pages were well instructed, and shewed every man his chamber, staying with us in another pallet, in case we wanted any thing. My chamber was royally furnished with rare tapistries, and hung about with paintings ; but above all things I was delighted in my Page, who was so ex-

Redduntur pondera choro Virginum.

2 Juvenes.

4 Virgines.

2 Virgines.

1 Virgo praestans.

The Dutchess.

Ponderum repositio in locum suum. The Dutchess.

Reginæ habitatio.

Supellex. The Dutchess.

Virgo lucifera discedit cubitum. Puerorum comitum officium. Autoris thalamus.

cellently spoken, and experienced in the arts, that he yet spent me another hour, and it was half an hour after three when I fell asleep. This was the first night that I slept in quiet, and yet a scurvy dream would not suffer me to rest, for I was troubled with a Door which I could not get open, though at last I did so. With these phantasies I passed the time, till at length, towards day, I awaked.

Somnium deporta difficili.

The Fourth Day.

I still lay in my bed, and leisurely surveighed the noble images and figures about my chamber, during which, on a sudden, I heard the musick of coronets, as if already they had been in procession. My Page skipped out of the bed as if he had been at his wits' end, and looked more like one dead than living. "The rest are already presented to the King," said he. I knew not what else to do but weep outright, and curse my own slothfulness. I dressed myself, but my Page was ready long before me, and ran out of the chamber to see how affairs might yet stand. He soon returned with the joyful news that the time was not past, only I had over-slept my breakfast, they being unwilling to waken me because of my age, but that now it was time for me to go with him to the Fountain, where most were assembled. With this consolation my spirit returned, wherefore I was soon ready with my habit, and went after the Page to the Fountain in the Garden, where I found that the Lyon, instead of his sword, had a pretty large tablet by him. Having well viewed it, I found that it was taken out of the ancient monuments, and placed here for some especial honour. The inscription was worn with age, and, therefore, I am minded to set it down here, as it is, and give every one leave to consider it.

Autor longiuscule dormiens expergesit.

Jentaculo privatur.

Leonis Tabula.

HERMES PRINCEPS.

POST TOT ILLATA
GENERI HUMANO DAMNA,

DEI CONSILIO:
ARTISQUE ADMINICULO
MEDICINA SALUBRIS FACTUS
HEIC FLUO.

Bibat ex me qui potest: lavet, qui vult: turbet, qui audet:
BIBITE FRATRES, ET VIVITE.

$$\infty \,) \,) \, : \, XX \,) \, IC \, \barA \, \cdots \, \text{w} \rightarrow \cdots$$

This writing might well be read and understood, being easier than any of the rest. After we had washed ourselves out of the Fountain, and every man had taken a draught out of an intirely golden cup, we once more followed the Virgin into the hall, and there put on new apparel, all of cloth of gold gloriously set out with flowers. There was also given to everyone another Golden Fleece, set about with pretious stones, and various workmanship according to the utmost skill of each artificer. On it hung a weighty medal of gold, whereupon were figured the sun and moon in opposition, but on the other side stood this poesie:—"The light of the moon shall be as the light of the sun, and the light of the sun shall be seven times brighter than at present." Our former jewels were laid in a little casket, and committed to one of the waiters. After this the Virgin led us out in our order, where the musitians waited ready at the door, all apparelled in red velvet

Scriptura facilis.

Potus.

Vestitus.

Clinodiæ.

Musici.

with white guards. After which a door, that I never before saw open, was unlocked; it opened on the Royal winding-stairs. There the Virgin led us, together with the musick, up three hundred sixty-five stairs; we saw nothing but what was of extream costly and artificial workmanship; the further we went, the more glorious still was the furniture, until at the top we came under a painted arch, where the sixty virgins attended us, all richly apparelled. As soon as they had bowed to us, and we as well as we could had returned our reverence, the musitians were dispatched away down the winding-stairs, the Door being shut after them. Then a little Bell was told, when in came a beautiful Virgin, who brought every one a wreath of lawrel, but our Virgins had branches given them. Meanwhile, a curtain was drawn up, where I saw the King and Queen as they sate in their majesty, and had not the yesterday queen warned me I should have equalled this unspeakable glory to Heaven; for besides that the room glittered of meer gold and pretious stones, the Queen's robes were so made that I was not able to behold them. In the meantime the Virgin stept in, and then each of the other virgins, taking one of us by the hand, with most profound reverence presented us to the King. Whereupon the Virgin began thus to speak:—"That to honour your most gratious, royal Majesties, these Lords have adventured hither with peril of body and life, your Majesties have reason to rejoyce, especially since the greatest part are qualified for inlarging your Majesties' dominions, as you will find by a most gratious particular examination of each. Herewith I was desirous thus to have them in humility presented to your Majesties, with most humble suit to discharge me of this my commission, and to take information from each of them concerning my actions and omissions."

Hereupon she laid her branch on the ground. It would have been fitting for one of us to have spoken somewhat on this occasion, but, seeing we were all troubled with the falling of the uvula, old Atlas stept forward and spoke on the King's behalf:—"Their Royal Majesties most gratiously rejoyce at your arrival, and will that their grace be assured to all. With thy administration, gentle Virgin, they are most gratiously satisfied, and a Royal Reward shall be provided for thee; yet it is their intention that thou shalt this day also continue with them, inasmuch as they have no reason to mistrust thee."

Here the Virgin humbly took up the branch, and we for this first time were to step aside with her. This room was square on the front, five times broader than it was long, but towards the West it had a great arch like a porch, where stood in circle three glorious thrones, the middlemost being somewhat higher than the rest. In each throne sate two persons—in the first sate a very antient King with a gray beard, yet his consort was extraordinarily fair and young. In the third throne sate a black King of middle age, and by him a dainty old matron, not crowned, but covered with a vail. But in the middle sate the two young persons, who though they had likewise wreaths of lawrel upon their heads, yet over them hung a large and costly crown. Now albeit they were not at this time so fair as I had before imagined to my self, yet so it was to be. Behind them on a round form sat for the most part antient men, yet none had any sword or other weapon about him. Neither saw I any life-guard but certain Virgins which were with us the day before, and who sate on the sides of the arch. I cannot pass in silence how the little Cupid flew to and again there, but for the most part he hovered about the great crown. Sometimes he seated himself in between the

Marginal notes:

Accessus ad regis aulam.

Laboratorium aronatum 60 Virgines.

Virg. Lucif.

Regis et Reginæ gloria.

Virgo lucifera præsentat hospites Regi.

Hospites nesciunt respondere. Atlas respondet.

Descriptio labatorii.

Subcellia.

1. Rex senex Conjux Juven.
2. Rex and conjux senes.

Scomna. assessores.

Cupide.

two lovers, somewhat smiling upon them with his bow. Sometimes he made as if he would shoot one of us; in brief, this knave was so full of his waggery, that he would not spare even the little birds, which in multitudes flew up and down the room, but tormented them all he could. The virgins also had their pastimes with him, and when they could catch him it was no easie matter for him to get from them again. Thus this little knave made all the sport and mirth. Before the Queen stood a small but inexpressibly curious altar, wherein lay a book covered with black velvet, only a little overlaid with gold. By this stood a taper in an ivory candlestick, which, although very small, burnt continually, and stood in that manner, that had not Cupid, in sport, now and then puffed upon it, we could not have conceived it to be fire. By this stood a sphere or celestial globe, which of itself turned about. Next this was a small striking-watch, by that a little christal pipe or syphon-fountain, out of which perpetually ran a clear blood-red liquor, and last of all there was a scull or death's head, in which was a white serpent, of such a length, that though she crept circle-wise about the rest of it, yet her taile still remained in one of the eye-holes until her head again entered at the other; so she never stirred from her scull, unless Cupid twitched a little at her, when she slipt in so suddenly that we could not choose but marvel at it. There were hung up and down the room wonderful images, which moved as if alive. Likewise, as we were passing out, there began such marvellous vocal musick that I could not tell whether it were performed by the virgins who yet stayed behind, or by the images themselves. We, being for this time satisfied, went thence with our virgins, who, the musitians, being already present, led us down the winding stairs, the door being diligently locked and bolted. As soon as we were come again into the hall, one of the virgins began:—"I wonder, Sister, that you durst adventure yourself amongst so many persons." "My Sister," replyed our president, "I am fearful of none so much as of this man," pointing at me. This speech went to my heart, for I understood that she mocked at my age, and indeed I was the oldest of all; yet she comforted me by promising, that in case I behaved myself well towards her, she would easily rid me of this burden.

Meantime, a collation was again brought in, and every one's Virgin seated by him, who well knew how to shorten the time with handsom discourses, but what these and their sports were I dare not blab out of school. Most of the questions were about the arts, whereby I could lightly gather that both young and old were conversant in the sciences. Still it run in my thoughts how I might become young again, whereupon I was somewhat the sadder. This the Virgin perceived, and, therefore, began:—"I dare lay anything, if I lye with him to-night, he shall be pleasanter in the morning." Hereupon they began to laugh, and albeit I blushed all over, I was fain to laugh too at my own ill-luck. Now there was one there that had a mind to return my disgrace upon the Virgin, whereupon he said:—"I hope not only we but the virgins themselves will bear witness, that our Lady President hath promised herself to be his bed-fellow to-night." "I should be well content with it," replyed the Virgin, "if I had not reason to be afraid of these my sisters; there would be no hold with them should I choose the best and handsomest for myself." "My Sister," presently began another, "we find hereby that thy high office makes thee not proud, wherefore if by thy permission we might by lot part the Lords here present, thou shouldst, with our goodwill, have such a prerogative." We let this pass for a jest, and began again to discourse together, but our Virgin could not leave tormenting us, and continued:—"My lords, how if we should permit fourtune to decide which of us must be together to-night?" "Well," said I, "if it may be no otherwise, we cannot refuse such a proffer." Now because it was concluded to make this trial after meat, we resolved to sit no longer at table, so we arose and each walked up and down with his Virgin. "Nay," said the president, "it shall not be so yet, let us see how fortune will couple us," upon which we were separated. Now first arose a dispute how the business should be carried out, but this was only a premeditated device, for the Virgin instantly proposed that we should mix ourselves in a ring, and that she beginning to count from herself, the seventh was to be content with the following seventh, were it a virgin or man. We were not aware of any craft, and therefore permitted it so to be; but when we thought we had very well mingled ourselves, the Virgins were so subtil that each knew her station before-hand. The president began to reckon, the seventh next her was a Virgin, the third seventh a Virgin likewise, and this continued till, to our amazement, all the Virgins came forth and none of us was hit. Thus we poor wretches remained standing alone, and were forced to confess that we had been handsomely couzened, albeit, whoever had seen us in our order might sooner have expected the sky to fall then that it should never have come to our turn. Herewith our sport was abandoned. In the interim the little wanton Cupid came also in unto us, but because he presented himself on behalf of their Royal Majesties, and delivered us a health from them out of a golden cup, and was to call our Virgin to the King, withal declaring he could not at this time tarry, we could not sport ourselves with him, so, with a due return of our most humble thanks we let him flye forth again. Now because the mirth began to fall into my consort's feet, and the Virgins were nothing sorry to see it, they lead up a civil dance which I rather beheld with pleasure than assisted, for my mercurialists were so ready with their postures, as if they had been long of the trade. After some few dances, our president came in again, and told us how the artists and students had offered themselves to their Royal Majesties before their departure to act a merry comedy; and if we thought good to be present thereat, and to waite upon their Royal Majesties to the House of the Sun, it would be acceptable to them. Hereupon we returned our humble thanks for the honour vouchsafed us, and most submissively tendered our small service, which the Virgin related, and presently brought word to attend their Royal Majesties in the gallery, whither we were soon led, and staid not long there, for the Royal Procession was just ready, yet without musick. The unknown Queen who was yesterday with us went foremost with a small and costly coronet, apparelled in white satin, and carrying nothing but a small crucifix made of a pearl, and this very day wrought between the young King and his Bride. After her went the six fore-mentioned Virgins in two ranks, carrying the King's jewels belonging to the little altar. Next to these came the three Kings. The Bridegroom was in the midst of them with a plain dress of black satin, after the Italian mode. He had on a small round black hat, with a little black pointed feather, which he courteously put off to us, thereby to signify his favour towards us. To him we bowed, as we had been before instructed. After the Kings came the three Queens, two whereof were richly habited; she in the middle went likewise all in black, and Cupid held up her train. Intimation was given us to follow, and after us the Virgins, old Atlas bringing up the rear. Through many stately walks we came to the House of the

Ludicra electio una dormientium.

A merry dance.

Hospites invitantur a virgine Lucif. ad comediam.

Processus Regis ad spectandum comediam.

Statio
spectatorum.

A Præcipuâ
quæ age-
bantur.

Actus 1.

Interludium.

Actus 2.

Actus 3.

Interludium.

Actus 4.

Sun. there next to the King and Queen, upon a richly furnished scaffold, to behold the foreordained comedy. We, though separa:ed, stood on the right hand of the Kings, but the Virgins on the left, except those to whom the Royal Ensignes were committed. To them was allotted a peculiar standing at top of all, but the rest of the attendants were content to stand below between the columns. Now because there are many remarkable passages in this Comedy, I will in brief run it over.

First of all came forth a very antient King with some servants: before his throne was brought a little chest, with mention that it was found upon the water. Being opened, there appeared in it a lovely babe, together with certain jewels, and a small parchment sealed, and superscribed to the King. This the King presently opened, and having read it, he wept and declared to his servants how injuriously the King of the **Moores** had deprived his aunt of her country, and had extinguished all the royal seed even to this infant, with the Daughter of which country he had purposed to match his Son. Hereupon he swore to maintain perpetual enmity with the Moore and his allies, and to revenge this on him. He commanded that the Child should be tenderly nursed, and to make preparations against the Moore. This provision, and the discipline of the young lady (who after she was a little grown up was committed to an ancient tutor), continued all the first act, with many laudable sports beside. In the interlude a Lyon and Griffon were set at one another, and the Lyon got the victory; this was also a pretty sight.

In the second act, the Moore, a black, treacherous fellow, came forth, who having with vexation understood that his murder was discovered, and that a little lady was craftily stollen from him, began to consult how by stratagem he might encounter so powerful an adversary, whereof he was at length advised by certain fugitives who fled to him through famine. So the young lady, contrary to all expectation, fell again into his hands, whom had he not been wonderfully deceived by his own servants, he had like to have slain. Thus this act was concluded with a mervelous triumph of the Moore.

In the third act a great army on the King's part was raised against the Moore, and put under the conduct of an antient, valiant knight, who fell into the Moore's country, till he forceably rescued the young Lady from a tower, and apparelled her anew. After this they erected a glorious scaffold and placed her upon it; presently came twelve royal embassadors, amongst whom the Knight made a speech, alledging that the King, his most gracious Lord, had not only heretofore delivered her from death, and caused her to be royally brought up, though she had not behaved herself altogether as became her, but, moreover, had, before others, elected her as a spouse for the young Lord, his Son, most gratiously desiring that the espousals might be really executed in case they would be sworn to his Majesty upon the following articles. Hereupon out of a patent he caused certain glorious conditions to be read; the young Lady took an oath inviolably to observe the same, returning thanks in most seemly sort for so high a grace. Whereupon they began to sing to the praise of God, of the King, and the young Lady, and for this time so departed. In sport, meanwhile, the four beasts of **Daniel**, as he saw them in the vision, were brought in, all which had its certain signification.

In the fourth act the young Lady was restored to her lost kingdom and crowned, being in this array conducted about the place with extraordinary joy. After various embassadors presented themselves not only to wish her prosperity but also to behold her glory. Yet it was not long that she preserved her integrity, but began to look wantonly about her, and to wink at the embassadors and lords. These her manners were soon known to the Moore, who would by no means neglect such an opportunity; and because her steward had not sufficient regard to her, she was easily blinded with great promises, so that she had no good confidence in her King, but privily submitted herself to the intire disposal of the Moore, who having by her consent gotten her into his hands, he gave her words so long till all her kingdom had subjected itself to him; after which, in the third scene of this act, he caused her to be led forth, stript naked, and then upon a scurvy wooden scaffold bound to a post, well scourged, and at last sentenced to death. This woful spectacle made the eyes of many to run over. Naked as she was, she was cast into prison, there to expect death by poyson, which, however, killed her not, but made her leprous all over. Thus this act was for the most part lamentable. Between they brought forth 𝕹𝖊𝖇𝖚𝖈𝖍𝖆𝖉𝖓𝖊𝖟𝖟𝖆𝖗'𝖘 image, which was adorned with all manner of arms on the head, breast, legs, and feet, of which more shall be spoken in the future explication.

In the fifth act the young King was acquainted with all that had passed between the Moore and his future spouse, who interceded with his father for her, intreating that she might not be left in that condition, and embassadors were dispatched to comfort her, but withal to give her notice of her inconsiderateness. She, nevertheless, would not receive them, but consented to be the Moore's concubine, and the young King was acquainted with it. After this comes a band of fools, each of which brought a cudgel, wherewith they made a great globe of the world, and undid it again, the which was a fine sportive phantsie.

Actus 5.

Interludium.

In the sixth act, the young King resolved to bid battle to the Moore, which was done, and albeit the Moore was discomfited, yet all held the young King for dead, but he came again to himself, released his spouse, and committed her to his steward and chaplain, the first whereof tormented her mightily, while the priest was so insolently wicked that he would needs be above all, till the same was reported to the young King, who dispatched one to break the neck of the priest's mightiness, and adorn the bride in some measure for the nuptials. After this act a vast artificial elephant was brought in, carrying a great tower with musitians, which was well pleasing to all.

Actus 6.

Interludium.

In the last act the bride-groom appeared in such pomp as is not well to be believed. The bride met him in the like solemnity, whereupon all the people cried out—VIVAT SPONSUM, VIVAT SPONSA, so that by this comedy they did withal congratulate our King and Queen in the most stately manner, which pleased them most extraordinary well. At length they made some pasces about the stage, till at last they altogether began thus to sing.

Actus 7.

Comædorum applausus erga Regem et Reginam.

I.

This time full of love
Does our joy much approve
Because of the King's Nuptial;
And, therefore, let's sing,
Till from all parts it ring,
Blest be he that granted us all!

Cantilena.

II.

The Bride most exquisitely faire,
Whom we attended long with care,
   To him in troth is plighted ;
We fully have at length obtain'd
The same for which we did contend—
   He's happy that's fore-sighted.

III.

Now the parents kind and good
By intreaties are subdued ;
Long enough in hold was she mew'd ;
   So in honour increase
   Till 𝕿𝖍𝖔𝖚𝖘𝖆𝖓𝖉𝖘 arise
And spring from your own proper blood.

Epilogus.

Hospites invitantur ad cœnam Regis et Reginæ.

Rex Adolesc.

Reges adulti.

Ordo discumbarium.

Ornatus vestium.

Corona super mensam.

Cupido was the merriest.

Sermones breves.

Oratio Regis adolescentis.

Haustus de silentio.

After this thanks were returned, and the comedy was finished with joy to the particular liking of the Royal Persons, who, the evening being already hard by, departed in their fore-mentioned order, we attending them up the winding stairs into the previous hall, where the tables were already richly furnished. This was the first time that we were invited to the King's table. The little altar was placed in the midst of the hall, and the six royal ensignes were laid upon it. The young King behaved himself very gratiously towards us, yet he could not be heartily merry ; he discoursed a little with us, yet often sighed, at which the little Cupid only mocked, and played his waggish tricks. The old King and Queen were very serious, but the wife of one of the ancient Kings was gay enough, the cause whereof I understood not. The Royal Persons took up the first table, at the second we only sate ; at the third some of the principal Virgins placed themselves. The rest were fain to wait. This was performed with such state and solemn stillness that I am afraid to make many words of it. All the Royal Persons, before meat, attired themselves in snow-white sufficiently illuminated the hall. All the lights were kindled at the pretious stones whereof, without other light, would have sufficiently illuminated the hall. All the lights were kindled at the small taper upon the altar. The young king frequently sent meat to the white serpeut, which caused me to muse. Almost all the prattle at this banquet was made by Cupid, who could not leave us, and me especially, untormented, and was perpetually producing some strange matter. However, there was no considerable mirth, from whence I could imagine some great imminent peril. There was no musick heard, and if we were demanded anything, we were fain to give short answers and so let it rest. In short, all things had so strange a face that the sweat began to trickle down over my body, and I believe that the stoutest-hearted man would have lost courage. Supper being almost ended, the young King commanded the book to be reached him from the altar. This he opened and caused it again to be propounded to us by an old man whether we resolved to abide with him in prosperity and adversity, which we having with trembling consented to, he further caused us sadly to be demanded whether we would give him our hands on it, which, when we could fain no reason, was fain so to be. One after another rose and with his own hand writ himself down in this book, after which the little christal fountain was brought near, together with a very small christal glass, out of which all the Royal Persons drank ; afterwards it was reached to us, and so forward to all, and this was called the Draught of Silence. Hereupon all the Royal Persons presented us their hands, declaring that in case we did not now stick to them we should never hereafter see them, which verily made our eyes run over. But our president engaged herself and promised largely on our behalf, which gave them satisfaction. Mean time a little bell was tolled, at which all the Royal Persons waxed so mighty bleak that we were ready utterly to despair. They quickly put off their white garments and assumed intirely black ones; the whole hall was hung with black velvet, the floor covered with the same, with which also the ceiling was over-spread. The tables were also removed, all seated themselves upon the form, and we also had put on black habits. Our president, who was before gone out, comes in again, bearing six black taffeta scarffs, with which she bound the six Royal Persons' eyes, and there were immediately brought in by the servants six covered coffins, which were set down, a low black seat being placed in their midst. Finally, there stept in a cole-black, tall man, who bare in his hand a sharp ax. Now after that the old King had been brought to the seat, his head was instantly whipt off and wrapped in a black cloth, the blood being received in a great golden goblet, and placed with him in the coffin that stood by, which, being covered, was set aside. Thus it went with the rest, so that I thought it would have come to me too, but as soon as the six Royal Persons were beheaded, the black man retired, another following who just before the door beheaded him also, and brought back his head, which, with the ax, was laid in a little chest. This indeed seemed to me a bloody Wedding, but, because I could not tell what the event would be, I was fain to captivate my under-standing until I were further resolved. The Virgin, seeing that some of us were faint-hearted and wept, bid us be content, saying:—"The life of these standeth now in your hands, and in case you follow me, this death shall make many alive."

Herewith she intimated we should go sleep and trouble our-selves no further, for they should have their due right. She bade us all good night, saying that she must watch the dead corps. We then were conducted by our Pages into our lodgings. My Page talked with me of sundry matters, and gave me cause enough to admire his understanding, but his intention was to lull me asleep, which at last I observed, whereupon I made as though I was fast asleep, but no sleep came to my eyes, and I could not put the beheaded out of my mind. Now my lodging was directly over against the great lake, so that I could look upon it, the win-dows being nigh the bed. About midnight I espied on the lake a great fire, wherefore I quickly opened the window to see what would become of it. Then from far I saw seven ships making forward all full of lights. Above each of them hovered a flame that passed to and fro, and sometimes descended, so that I could lightly judge that it must needs be the spirits of the beheaded. The ships gently approached to land, and each had no more than one mariner. When they were gotten to shore, I espied our Virgin with a torch going towards them, after whom the six covered coffins, together with the little chest, were carried, and each was privily laid in a ship. Wherefore I awaked my Page, who hugely thanked me, for having run much up and down all day, he might quite have over-slept this, though he well knew it. As soon as the coffins were laid in the ships, all the lights were extinguished, and the six flames passed back together over the lake, so that there was but one light for a watch in each ship. There were also some hundreds of watchmen encamped on the shore, who sent the Virgin back again into the Castle, she carefully bolting all up again; so that I could judge that there was nothing more to be done this night. We again betook ourselves to rest. I only

Fide jubetur virg. luci.

Mors Regulorum.

Decollatio Regum.

Carnificis.

Hospites mærent. Solatium.

Cura nocturna mortuorum.

Cubiculum. Visio nocturna.

Cadavera avehuntur trans Lacum.

Autor solus
hæc vidit.
of all my company had a chamber towards the lake and saw this. Then being extream weary I fell asleep in my manifold speculations.

The Fifth Day.

Obambulatio
antelucana.
The night was over, and the dear wished-for day broken, when hastily I got me out of bed, more desirous to learn what might insue than that I had sufficiently slept. After I had put on my cloathes, and according to my custom was gone down stairs, it was still too early, and I found nobody else in the hall, wherefore I entreated my Page to lead me a little about the castle, and shew me somewhat that was rare, who now (as always) willing, presently lead me down certain steps underground to a great iron door, on which the following words were fixed in large copper letters :—

L

Thalamus
veneris
sepultæ.
These I copied and set down in my table-book. After this door was opened, the Page lead me by the hand through a very dark passage till we came to a little door now only put too, for, as the Page informed me, it was first opened yesterday when the coffins were taken out, and had not since been shut. As soon as we stepped in I espied the most pretious thing that Nature ever created, for this vault had no other light but from certain huge carbuncles. Thesaurus
Regis. This was the King's Treasury, but the most glorious and principal thing was a sepulchre in the middle, so rich that I wondered it was no better guarded, whereunto the Page answered me, that I had good reason to be thankful to my planet, by whose influence I had now seen certain pieces which no humane eye (except those of the King's family) had ever viewed. Descriptio
sepulchri. This sepulcher was triangular, and had in the middle of it a kettle of polished copper, the rest was of pure gold and pretious stones. In the kettle stood an angel, who held in his arms an unknown tree, whose fruit continually falling into the kettle, turned into water therein, and ran out into three small golden kettles standing by. This little altar was supported by an eagle, an ox, and a lion, which stood on an exceeding costly base. I asked my Page what this might signifie. "Here," said he, "lies buried Lady Venus, that beauty which hath undone many a great man, both in fourtune, honour, blessing, and prosperity"; after which he showed me a copper door in the pavement, saying, "Here, if you Aliud triclinium. please, we may go further down." We descended the steps, where it was exceeding dark, but the Page immediately opened a little chest in which stood a small ever-burning taper, wherefrom he kindled one of the many torches that lay by. I was mightily terrified and asked how he durst do this. He gave me for answer, "as long as the Royal Persons are still at rest I have nothing to fear." Herewith I espied a rich bed ready made, hung about with

curious curtains, one of which he drew, and I saw the Lady Venus stark naked (for he heaved up the coverlets too), lying there in such beauty, and a fashion so surprising, that I was almost besides myself, neither do I yet know whether it was a piece thus carved, or an humane corps that lay dead there, for she was altogether immoveable, and yet I durst not touch her. So she was again covered, yet she was still, as it were, in my eye. But I soon espyed behind the bed a tablet on which it was thus written.

Descriptio corporis veneris dormientis.

I asked my Page concerning this writing, but he laughed, with promise that I should know it too, and, he putting out the torch, we again ascended. Then I better viewed all the little doors, and found that on every corner there burned a small tayper of pyrites of which I had before taken no notice, for the fire was so clear that it looked much liker a stone than a taper. From this heat the tree was forced continually to melt, yet it still produced new fruit. "Now, behold," said the Page, "when the tree shall be quite melted down, then shall Lady Venus awake and be the mother of a King." Whilst he was thus speaking, in flew the little Cupid, who at first was somewhat abashed at our presence, but seeing us both look more like the dead then the living, he could not refrain from laughing, and demanded what spirit had brought me thither, whom I with trembling answered, that I had lost my way in the castle, and was by chance come hither, that the Page had likewise been looking up and down for me, and at last lited upon me here, and that I hoped he would not take it amiss. "Nay, then, 'tis well enough yet," said Cupid, "my old busie gransir, but you might lightly have served me a scurvy trick, had you been aware of this door. I must look better to it," and so he put a strong lock on the copper door where we before descended. I thanked God that he lited upon us no sooner; my Page, too was the more jocond because I had so well helped him at this pinch. "Yet can I not," said Cupid, "let it pass unrevenged that you were so near stumbling upon my dear mother." With that he put the point of his dart into one of the little tapers, and heating it somewhat, pricked me with it on the hand, which at that time I little regarded, but was glad that it went so well with us. Meantime my companions were gotten out of bed and were come into the hall, to whom I joyned myself, making as if I were then first risen. After Cupid had carefully made all fast again, he came likewise to us, and would needs have me shew him my hand, where he still found a little drop of blood, at which he heartily laughed, and bad the rest have a care of me, as I would shortly end my days. We all wondered how he could be so merry

Arboris calor ex facibus

Mulcta facta hujus obambulationis.

Cupido illudit autori.

and have no sence of yesterday's sad passages. Our President had meantime made herself ready for a journey, coming in all in black velvet, yet she and her Virgins still bare their branches of lawrel. All things being in readiness, she bid us first drink somewhat, and then presently prepare for the procession, wherefore we made no long tarrying, but followed her out of the hall into the court, where stood six coffins and my companions thought no other but that the six Royal Persons lay in them, but I well observed the device though I knew not what was to be done with these other. By each coffin were eight muffled men. As soon as the musick went, it was so doleful a tune that I was astonished at it, they took up the coffins, and we followed them into the Garden, in the midst of which was erected a wooden edifice, have round about the roof a glorious crown, and standing upon seven columns. Within it were formed six sepulchers; by each of them was a stone, but in the middle it had a round hollow rising stone. In these graves the coffins were quietly, and with many ceremonies, laid; the stones were shoved over them, and they shut fast, but the little chest was to lie in the middle. Herewith were my companions deceived, for they imagined that the dead corps were there. On the top of all was a great flag, having a Phœnix painted on it, perhaps the more to delude us. After the funerals were done, the Virgin, having placed herself upon the midmost stone, made a short oration, exhorting us to be constant to our ingagements, not to repine at the pains we must undergo, but be helpful in restoring the buried Royal Persons to life, and therefore, without delay, to rise and make a journey with her to the Tower of Olympus, to fetch thence the medicines necessary for this purpose.

This we soon agreed to, and followed her through another little door to the shore, where the seven ships stood empty, and on them all the Virgins stuck up their Laurel branches, and, having distributed us in the six ships, they caused us in God's name to begin our voyage, and looked upon us as long as we were in sight, after which they, with all the watchmen, returned to the Castle. Our ships had each of them a peculiar device; five of them, indeed, had the five regular bodies, each a several one, but mine, in which the Virgin too sate, carried a globe. Thus we sailed on in a singular order, and each had only two mariners. Foremost went the ship a in which, as I conceive, the Moor lay. In this were twelve musitians who played excellently well, and its device was a pyramid. Next followed three abreast, b, c, and d, in which we were disposed; I sate in c. Behind these came the two fairest and stateliest ships, e and f, stuck about with many branches of lawrel,

and having no passengers in them; their flags were the sun and moon. But in the rear was only one ship, g, and in this were forty Virgins. Having passed over this lake, we came through a narrow arm into the right sea, where all the sirens, nymphs, and sea-goddesses attended us, and immediately dispatched a sea-nymph unto us to deliver their present of honour to the Wedding. It was a costly, great, set, round, and orient pearl, the like to which hath not at any time been seen, either in ours or in the new world. The Virgins having friendly received it, the nymph intreated that audience might be given to their divertisements, which the Virgin was content to give, and commanded the two great ships to stand into the middle,

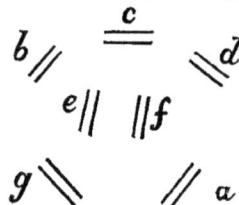

and to the rest to incompass them in pentagon, after which the nymphs fell into a ring about them, and with a most delicate sweet voice began thus to sing:

I.

There's nothing better here below
Than beauteous, noble Love,
Whereby we like to God do grow,
And none to grief do move;
Wherefore let's chant it to the King,
That all the sea therewith may ring.
We question, answer you !

II.

What was it that at first us made?
'Twas Love.
And what hath grace afresh conveigh'd?
'Twas Love.
And whence (pray tell us !) were we born ?
Of Love.
How came we then again forlorn ?
Sans Love.

III.

Who was it, say, that us conceived ?
'Twas Love.
Who suckled, nursed, and relieved ?
'Twas Love.
What do we to our parents owe ?
'Tis Love.
Why do they us such kindness show ?
Of Love.

IV.

Who gets herein the victory ?
'Tis Love.
Can Love by search obtained be?
By Love.
How may a man good works perform?
Through Love.
Who into on can two transform?
'Tis Love.

V.

Then let our song sound,
Till its eccho rebound,
To love's honour and praise ;
May it ever increase
With our noble Princes, the King and the Queen,
The soul is departed, their body's within.

VI.

And as long as we live
God gratiously give,
That as great love and amity
They bear each other mightily,
So we, likewise, by love's own flame
May reconjoyn them once again.

VII.

Then this annoy Into great joy
(If many thousand younglings deign)
Shall change, and ever so remain.

Autori perplacent nymphæ and cantus.

The nymphs rewarded.

Autori desunt adhuc duo.

Turris Olympi.

Custos.

Structura. Dies.

1. Conclave.

Labores hospitum.

Virginum.

Cibus Potus.

Lectus tenuis.

Autor speculatur cœlum prosomno.

These having, with most admirable concent and melody finished this song, I no more wondered at Ulisses for stopping the ears of his companions; I seemed to myself the most unhappy man alive that Nature had not made me too so trim a creature. But the Virgin soon dispatched them, and commanded to set sail; wherefore the nymphs, having been presented with a long red scarff for a gratuity, dispersed themselves in the sea. I was at this time sensible that Cupid began to work with me too, which tended little to my credit; but as my giddiness is likely to be nothing beneficial to the reader, I am resolved to let it rest. This was the wound that in the first book I received on my head in a dream. Let every one take warning by me of loitering about Venus's bed, for Cupid can by no means brook it. After some hours, we came within ken of the Tower of Olympus, wherefore the Virgin commanded by the discharge of some pieces to give signal of our approach, and immediately we espyed a great white flag thrust out, and a small gilded pinnace sent forth to meet us, wherein was a very antient man, the Warder of the Tower, with certain guards in white, by whom we were friendly received, and conducted to the Tower, which was situated upon an island exactly square,[1] and environed with a wall so firm and thick that I counted two hundred and sixty paces over. On the other side was a fine meadow with certain little gardens, in which grew strange, and to me unknown fruits. There was an inner wall about the Tower which itself was as if seven round towers had been built one by another, yet the middlemost was somewhat higher, and within they all entered one into another. Being come to the gates of the Tower, we were led a little aside on the wall, that so the coffins might be brought in without our notice, but of this the rest knew nothing. We were conducted into the Tower at the very bottom, which was an excellently painted laboratory, where we were fain to beat and wash plants, precious stones, and all sorts of things, extract their juice and essence, put up the same in glasses, and deliver them to be laid up. Our Virgin was so busie with us, and so full of directions, that she knew not how to give us employment enough, so that in this island we were meer drudges till we had atchieved all that was necessary for restoring the beheaded bodies. Meantime, as I afterwards learned, three Virgins were in the first apartment washing the corps with diligence. Having at length almost done our preparation, some broath, with a little draught of wine, was brought us, whereby I observed that we were not here for pleasure. When we had finished our day's work, everyone had a mattress laid on the ground for him, wherewith we were to content ourselves. For my part I was not much troubled with sleep, and walking out into the garden, at length came as far as the wall, where, the heaven being very clear, I could well give away the time in contemplating the stars. By chance I came to a great pair of stone stairs leading to the top of the wall, and because the moon shone very bright, I was so much the more confident, and, going up, looked too a little upon the sea, which was exceedingly calm. Thus having good opportunity to consider better of astronomy, I found that this night there would happen such a conjunction of the planets, the like to which was not otherwise suddenly to be observed. Having looked a good while into the sea, and it being just about midnight, I beheld from far the seven Flames passing over sea hitherward and betakeing themselves to the top of the spire of the tower. This made me somewhat affraid; for as soon as the Flames had settled themselves, the winds rose, and made the sea very tempestuous. The moon also was covered with

[1] See additional note, No. 4.

clouds, and my joy ended with such fear that I had scarce time enough to hit upon the stairs again, and betake myself to the Tower, where I laid myself down upon my mattress, and there being in the laboratory a pleasant and gently purling fountain, I fell asleep so much the sooner. And thus this fifth day too was concluded with wonders.

The Sixth Day.

Next morning, after we had awaked another, we sate together to discourse what might be the wont of things. Some were of opinion that the corps should all be inlivened again together. Others contradicted this, because the decease of the ancients was not only to restore life but increase too to the young ones. Some imagined that they were not put to death, but, that others were beheaded in their stead. Having talked a pretty while, in comes the old man, and first saluting us, looks about to see if all things were ready. We had herein so behaved ourselves that he had no fault to find with our diligence, whereupon he placed all the glasses together and put them into a case. Presently come certain youths bringing ladders, roapes, and large wings, which they laid before us and departed. Then the old man began thus :— "My dear Sons, one of these three things must each of you this day constantly bear about with him. It is free for you to make choice of one of them, or to cast lots." We replied that we would choose. "Nay," said he, "let it rather go by lot. Hereupon he made three little schedules, writing on one Ladder, on the second Rope, on the third Wings. These he laid in an hat; each man must draw, and whatever he happened on was to be his. Those who got ropes imagined themselves in the best case; but I chanced on a ladder, which hugely afflicted me, for it was twelve-foot long, pretty weighty, and I must be forced to carry it, whereas the others could handsomely coyle their ropes about them, and as for the wings, the old man joyned them so neatly on to the third sort as if they had grown upon them. Hereupon he turned the cock, and the fountain ran no longer, and we were fain to remove it out of the way. After all things were carried off, he, taking with him the casket and glasses, took leave, and locked the door after him so we imagined that we had been imprisoned in this Tower; but it was hardly a quarter of an hour before a round hole above was uncovered, where we saw our Virgin, who bad us good morrow, desiring us to come up. They with the wings were instantly through the hole; only they with the ropes were in an evil plight, for as soon as ever one of us was up, he was commanded to draw up the ladder to him. At last each man's rope was hanged on an iron hook, and he climbed up as well as he could, which indeed was not compassed without blisters. When we were all well up, the hole was again covered, and we were friendly received by the Virgin. This room was the whole breadth of the Tower itself, having six very stately vestries a little raised and reached by three steps. In these we were distributed to pray for the life of the King and Queen. Meanwhile the Virgin went in and out at the little door *a* till we had done. As soon as our process was absolved, there was brought in through the little door by twelve persons, which were formerly our musitians, a wonderful thing of longish shape, which my companions took to be a fountain, and which was placed in the middle. I well observed that the corps lay in it, for the inner chest was of an oval figure, so large that six persons might well lie therein one by another. After this they again went forth, fetched their instruments, and conducted in our Virgin, with her she-attendants,

(marginal notes)
Define ortæ dubiæ opiniones.

Custos. Pyrotechnia hospitum laudatur. Pueri armiferi.

Sors.

Acensus in 2 conclave.

Restis difficultas.

Descriptio 2 conclave.

The little
casket

to a most delicate voice of musick. The Virgin carried a little casket, the rest only branches, and small lamps or lighted torches which last were immediately given into our hands, and we stood about the fountain in this order.

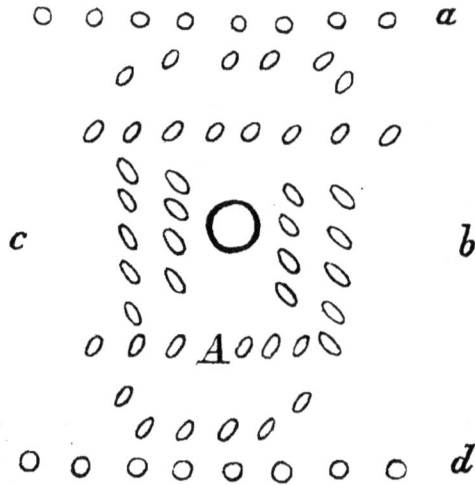

Ordo chori.

Virgines
unde.

Quid in
arcula.

First stood the Virgin A, with her attendants in a ring round about, with the lamps and branches *c*. Next stood we with our torches *b*, then the musitians in a long rank; last of all, the rest of the Virgins *d*, in another long rank. Whence the Virgins came, whether they dwelt in the Castle, or were brought in by night, I know not, for their faces were covered with delicate white linnen. The Virgin opened the casket, in which was a round thing wrapped in a piece of green double taffata. This she laid in the uppermost kettle, and covered it with the lid, which was full of holes, and had besides a rim, on which she poured in some of the water which we had the day before prepared; the fountain began immediately began to run, and through four small pipes to drive into the little kettle. Beneath the undermost kettle were many sharp points, on which the Virgins stuck their lamps, that the heat might come to the kettle and make the water seeth, which, when it began to simper, by many little holes at *a*, fell in upon the bodies, and was so hot that it dissolved them all, and turned them into liquor. What the abovesaid round wrapt-up thing was, my companions knew not, but I understood that it was the Moor's head, from which the water conceived so great heat. At *b*, round

Rami
laures.

about the great kettle, there were again many holes, in which they stuck their branches, but whether this was done of necessity or for ceremony I know not. However, these branches were continually sprinkled by the fountain, whence it afterwards dropt somewhat of a deeper yellow into the kettle. This lasted for near two hours, the fountain still running, but more faintly. Meantime the musitians went their way, and we walked up and down in the room, which truly was so made that we had opportunity enough to pass away our time. There were images, paintings, clock-works, organs, springing fountains, and the like. When it was near the time that the fountain ceased, the Virgin commanded a golden globe to be brought. At the bottom of the foun-

Deliciæ in
conclavi.

tain was a tap, by which she let out all the matter dissolved by
those hot drops (whereof certain quarts were then very red)
into the globe. The rest of the water above in the kettle was
poured out, and so this fountain was again carried forth. Whether
it was opened abroad, or whether anything of the bodies that was
useful yet remained, I dare not certainly say, but the water
emptied into the globe was much heavier than six or more of us
were able to bear, albeit for its bulk it should have seemed not
too heavy for one man. This globe being with much ado gotten out
of doors, we again sate alone, but I, perceiving a trampling overhead, had an eye to my ladder. After one-quarter of an hour,
the cover above was lifted, and we commanded to come up,
which we did as before, with wings, ladders, and ropes, and it did
not a little vex me that whereas the Virgins could go up another
way, we were fain to take so much toil; yet I could judge there
must be some special reason for it, and we must leave somewhat
for the old man to do too. The hole being again shut fast, I saw
the globe hanging by a strong chain in the middle of the room,
in which there was nothing but windows, with a door between
every two, which was covered with a great polished looking-glass.
These windows and looking-glasses were so optically opposed
that although the sun, which now shined exceeding bright, beat
only upon one door, yet (after the windows towards the sun were
opened, and the doors before the looking-glasses drawn aside)
in all quarters of the room there was nothing but suns, which
by artificial refractions beat upon the whole golden globe hanging
in the midst, which, being polished, gave such a lustre that none
of us could open our eyes but were forced to look out at windows
till the globe was well heated, and brought to the desired effect.
In these mirrors I saw the most wonderful spectacles that ever
nature brought to light, for there were suns in all places, and the
globe in the middle shined brighter yet. At length the virgin
commanded to shut up the looking-glasses and make fast the
windows to let the globe cool a little, wherefore we thought good,
since we might now have leisure, to refresh ourselves with a
breakfast. This treatment was again right philosophical, and we
had no need to be afraid of intemperance, though we had no
want, while the hope of the future joy, with which the virgin
continually comforted us, made us so jocond that we regarded
not any pains or inconvenience. I can truly say concerning my
companions of high quality that their minds never ran after their
kitchen or table, but their pleasure was only to attend on this
adventurous physic, and hence to contemplate the Creator's wisdom and omnipotency. After our reflection we settled ourselves
to work, for the globe was sufficiently cooled, which with toil
and labour we were to lift off the chain and set upon the floor.
The dispute then was how we were to get the globe in sunder,
for we were commanded to divide it in the midst. The conclusion was that a sharp-pointed diamond would be best to do it,
and when we had thus opened the globe, there was no redness to
be seen, but a lovely great snow-white egg, and it mightily rejoyced us that this was so well brought to pass, for the virgin was
in perpetual care least the shell might still be too tender. We
stood around about this egg as jocond as if we ourselves had laid
it, but the Virgin made it presently be carried forth, and departed herself, locking the door behind her. What she did abroad
with the egg, or whether it were privately handled, I know not,
neither do I believe it. We were again to pause for one quarter
of an hour, till the third hole opened, and we, by means of our
instruments, came upon the fourth stone or floor. In this room
we found a great copper kettle filled with silver sand which was

Gravitas aquæ.

Ascensus in 3 conclave.

Descriptio conclavis.

Artif. optica.

Mirac. spec.

Prandium philosoph.

warmed with a gentle fire, and afterwards the egg was raked up in it, that it might therein come to perfect maturity. This kettle was exactly square. Upon one side stood these two verses writ in great letters—

O. BLI. TO. BIT. MI. LI.
KANT. I.[1] VOLT. BIT. TO. GOLT.

On the second side were these three words—

SANITAS. NIX. HASTA.

The third had but this one word—

F.I.A.T.

But on the hindmost part stood an entire inscription running thus—

QUOD
Ignis: Aer: Aqua: Terra:
SANCTIS REGUM ET REGI-
NABUM NOSTR:
Cineribus
Eripere non potuerunt.
Fidelis Chymicorum Turba
IN HANC URNAM
Contulit.
A*o*

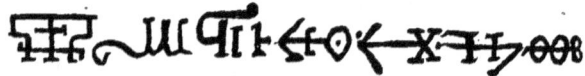

Now, whether the sand or egg were hereby meant I leave the learned to dispute. Our egg, being ready, was taken out, but it needed no cracking, for the Bird soon freed himself, looking very jocond, though bloody and unshapen. We first set him on the warm sand, the Virgin commanding that before we gave him anything to eat we should be sure to make him fast, otherwise he would give us all work enough. This being done, food was brought him, which surely was nothing but the blood of the beheaded deluted with prepared water, by which the Bird grew so fast under our eye that we well saw why the Virgin gave such warning of him. He bit and scratched so devilishly that, could he have had his will upon any of us, he would soon have dispatched him. Now he was wholly black and wild, wherefore other meat was brought him, perhaps the blood of another of the Royal Persons, whereupon all his black feathers moulted and were replaced by snow-white ones. He was somewhat tamer too, and more tractable, though we did not yet trust him. At the third feeding his feathers began to be so curiously coloured that I never saw the like for beauty. He was also exceedingly tame, and behaved himself so friendly with us that, the Virgin consenting, we released him from captivity. "'Tis now reason," she began, "since by your diligence, and our old man's consent, the Bird has attained with his life and the highest perfection, that he be also joyfully consecrated by us." Herewith she commanded to bring in dinner, since

Pullus implumis.

*Vincitur.
Pascitur sanguine decallatorum.*

Sanguine alius Regis pascitur.

Iridescit.

Liberatur vinculis.

---

[1] This letter is omitted in one of the German editions.

the most troublesome part of our work was now over, and it was fit we should begin to enjoy our passed labours. We began to make merry together. Howbeit, we had still our mourning cloaths on, which seemed somewhat reproachful to our mirth. The Virgin was perpetually inquisitive, perhaps to find to which of us her future purpose might prove serviceable, but her discourse was, for the most part, about Melting, and it pleased her well when any one seemed expert in such compendious manuals as do peculiarly commend an artist. This dinner lasted not above three-quarters of an hour, which we yet, for the most part, spent with our Bird, whom we were fain constantly to feed with his meat, though he continued much at the same growth. After Dinner we were not long suffered to digest our food, for the Virgin, together with the Bird, departed from us, and the fifth room was opened, which we reached after the former manner, and tendred our service. In this room a bath was prepared for our Bird, which was so coloured with a white powder that it had the appearance of milk. It was cool when the Bird was set into it, and he was mighty well pleased with it, drinking of it and pleasantly sporting in it. But after it began to heat, by reason of the lamps placed under it, we had enough to do to keep him in the bath. We, therefore, clapt a cover on the kettle, and suffered him to thrust out his head through a hole, till he had lost all his feathers in this bath, and was as smooth as a new-born babe, yet the heat did him no further harm. In this bath the feathers were quite consumed, and the bath was thereby turned into blew. At length we gave the Bird air, who of himself sprung out of the kettle, and was so glitteringly smooth that it was a pleasure to behold him. But because he was still somewhat wild, we were fain to put a collar, with a chain, about his neck, and so led him up and down the room. Meantime a strong fire was made under the kettle, and the bath sodden away till it all came to a blew stone, which we took out, and having pounded it, we ground it on a stone, and finally with this colour painted the Bird's whole skin over, who then looked much more strangely, for he was all blew, except the head, which remained white. Herewith our work in this story was performed, and we, after the Virgin with her blew Bird was departed from us, were called up a hole to the sixth story, where we were mightily troubled, for in the midst a little altar, every way like that in the King's hall, was placed. Upon it stood the six forementioned particulars and he himself (the Bird) made the seventh. First of all the little fountain was set before him, out of which he drunk a good draught; afterwards he pecked upon the white serpent till she bled mightily. This blood we received in a golden cup, and poured down the Bird's throat, who was mighty averse from it; then we dipt the serpent's head in the fountain, upon which she again revived, and crept into her death's head, so that I saw her no more for a long time. Meanwhile the sphere turned constantly on until it made the desired conjunction. Immediately the watch struck one, upon which there was going another conjunction. Then the watch struck two. Finally, whilst we were observing the third conjunction, and the same was indicated by the watch, the poor Bird himself submissively laid down his neck upon the book, and willingly suffered his head to be smitten off by one of us, thereto chosen by lot. Howbeit he yielded not one drop of blood till he was opened on the breast, and then the blood spun out so fresh and clear as if it had been a fountain of rubies. His death went to the heart of us, yet we might well judge that a naked bird would stand us in little stead. We removed the little altar, and assisted the Virgin to burn the body, together with the little tablet hanging by, to ashes, with fire kindled at the little taper, afterwards to cleanse the same several times, and to lay them in a box of cypress

Primus usus ejus.

Μεθοδία

5 Conclave.

Avis balneum.

Vincitur.

Balneum coquitur in lapidem.

6 Conclave.

Avis decollatur.

Avis combursitur.

Jocus.

wood. Here I cannot conceal what a trick I, with three more, was served. After we had diligently taken up the ashes, the Virgin began to speak thus:—"My Lords, we are here in the sixth room, and have only one more before us, in which our trouble will be at an end, and we shall return home to our castle to awaken our most gratious Lords and Ladies. Now albeit I could heartily wish that all of you had behaved yourselves in such a sort that I might have given your commendations to our most renowned King and Queen, and you have obtained a suitable reward, yet because, contrary to my desire, I have found amongst you these four"—pointing at me and three others—"lazy and sluggish labourators, and yet according to my good will to all, I am not willing to deliver them to condign punishment. However, that such negligence may not remain wholly unpunished, I purpose that they shall be excluded from the future seventh and most glorious action of all the rest, and so they shall incur no further blame from their Royal Majesties."

In what a case we now were I leave others to consider, for the Virgin so well knew how to keep her countenance that the water soon ran over baskets, and we esteemed ourselves the most unhappy of all men. The Virgin, by one of her maids, whereof there were many always at hand, caused the musitians to be fetcht, who were with cornets to blow us out of doors with such scorn and derision that they themselves could hardly sound for laughing. But it did particularly afflict us that the Virgin vehemently laughed at our weeping, and that there might be some amongst our companions who were glad of our misfortune. But it proved otherwise, for as soon as we were come out at the door the musitians bid us be of good cheere, and follow them up the winding staires to the eighth floor under the roof, where we found the old man standing upon a little round furnace. He received us friendly, and heartily congratulated us that we were hereto chosen by the Virgin; but after he had understood the fright we had conceived, his belly was ready to burst with laughing that we had taken such good fortune so hainously. "Hence," said he, "my dear sons, learn that man never knoweth how well God intendeth him." The Virgin also came running in, who, after she had sufficiently laughed at us, emptied her ashes into another vessel, filling hers again with other matter, saying, she must now cast a mist before the other artist's eyes, that we in the mean time should obey the old lord, and not remit our former diligence. Herewith she departed from us into the seventh room, whither she called our companions. What she first did with them I cannot tell, for they were not only most earnestly forbidden to speak of it, but we, by reason of our business, durst not peep on them through the ceiling. Our work was to moisten the ashes with our fore-prepared water till they became a very thin dough, after which we set the matter over the fire till it was well heated; then we cast it into two little forms or moulds, and so let it cool a little when we had leisure to look on our companions through certain crevises in the floor. They were busie at a furnace, and each was himself fain to blow up the fire with a pipe, till he was ready to lose his breath. They imagined they were herein wonderfully preferred before us. This blowing lasted till our old man rouzed us to work again. We opened our little forms, and there appeared two bright and almost transparent little images, a male and a female, the like to which man's eye never saw, each being but four inches long, and that which most mightily surprised me was that they were not hard, but limber and fleshy as other human bodies; yet they had no life, so that I assuredly believe that Lady Venus' image was made after some such way. These angelically fair babes we laid upon two little sattin cushonets, and beheld them till we were almost besotted

Commodum ejoco.

8. Conclave.

Virgo. lucif. ludit cœteros.

7. Conclave.

Verus labor sub tecto.

Labor spurius in 7 conclavi.

Homunculi duo.

upon so exquisite an object. The old lord warned us to forbear, Pascuntur sanguine avis. and continually to instil the blood of the bird, which had been received in a little golden cup, drop after drop into the mouths of the little images, from whence they apparently encreased, becoming according to proportion much more beautiful. They grew so big that we lifted them from the little cushonets and were fain to lay them upon a long table covered with white velvet. The old man commanded us to cover them up to the breast with a piece of fine white double taffata, which, because of their unspeak- Pulcherrimus. able beauty, almost went against us. Before we had in this manner quite spent the blood, they were in their perfect full growth, having gold-yellow curled hair, and the figure of Venus was nothing to them. But there was not yet any natural warmth or acnai bility in them; they were dead figures, yet of a lively and natural colour; and since care was to be taken that they grew not too great, the old man would not permit anything more to be given them, but covered their faces too with the silk, and caused the table to be stuck round about with torches. Let the reader imagine not these lights to have been of necessity, for the old man's intent was that we should not observe when the Soul entered into them, as indeed we should not have taken notice of it, in case I had not twice before seen the flames. However, I permitted the other three to remain in their belief, neither did the old man know that I had seen anything more. Hereupon he bid us sit down on a bench over against the table. The Virgin came in with the musick and all furniture, and carried two curious white garments, Vestiuntur. the like to which I had never seen in the Castle. I thought no other but that they were meer christal, but they were gentle and not transparent. These she laid upon a table, and after she had disposed her Virgins upon a bench round about, she and the old man began many *leger-de-main* tricks about the table, which were Spectatores luduntur. done only to blind. All this was managed under the roof, which was wonderfully formed, for on the inside it was arched into seven Descriptio tecti. hemispheres, of which the middlemost was somewhat the highest, and had at top a little round hole, which was shut and was observed by none but myself. After many ceremonies stept in six Virgins, each of which bare a large trumpet, rouled about with a green, glittering, and burning material like a wreath, one of which the old man took, and after he had removed some of the lights at top, and uncovered their faces, he placed one of the trumpets upon the mouth of one of the bodies in such manner that the upper and wider part of it was directed towards the fore- mentioned hole. Here my companions always looked upon the Usus tubarum. images, but as soon as the foliage or wreath about the shank of the trumpet was kindled, I saw the hole at top open and a bright Forti ex cœlo veniens. stream of fire shoot down the tube and pass into the body, whereupon the hole was again covered, and the trumpet removed. With this device my companions were deluded into imagining that life came to the image by the fire of the foliage, for as soon as he received his Soul he twinckled his eyes though scarcely stirring. The second time he placed another tube upon its mouth, kindled Homunculi animati alio transferuntur. it again, and the Soul was let down through the tube. This was repeated upon each of them three times, after which all the lights were extinguished and carried away. The velvet carpets of the table were cast together over them, and immediately a travelling bed was unlocked and made ready, into which thus wrapped up, they were born, and, after the carpets were taken off them, neatly laid by each other, where, with the curtains drawn before them, they slept a good while. It was now time for the Virgin to see how De. 7 concl. the other artists believed themselves; they were well pleased because they were to work in gold, which is indeed a piece of this art, but not the most principal, necessary, and best. They had too a part of these ashes, so they imagined that the whole Bird was provided for the sake of gold, and that life must thereby be restored to the deceased. Mean time we sate very still, attending when our married couple would awake, and thus about half an hour was spent. Then the wanton Cupid presented himself, and, after he had saluted us all, flew to them behind the curtain, tormenting them till they waked. This happened to them with very great amazement, for they imagined that they had slept from the hour in which they were beheaded. Cupid, after he had awaked them, and renewed their acquaintance one with another, stepped aside and permitted them to recruit their strength, mean time playing his tricks with us, and at length he would needs have the musick fetcht to be somewhat the merrier. Not long after the Virgin herself comes, and after having most humbly saluted the young King and Queen, who found themselves somewhat faint, and having kissed their hands, she brought them the two forementioned curious garments, which they put on, and so stepped forth. There were already prepared two very curious chaires, wherein they placed themselves, and were by us with most profound reverence congratulated, for which the King in his own person most gratiously returned his thanks and again re-assured us of all grace. It was already about five of clock, wherefore they could make no longer stay; but as soon as ever the chiefest of their furniture could be laden, we were to attend the young Royal Persons down the stairs through all doors and watches unto the ship, in which they imbarqued together with certain Virgins and Cupid, and sailed so swiftly that we soon lost sight of them, yet they were met. as I was informed by certain stately ships, and in four hours time had made many leagues out at sea. After five of clock the musitians were charged to carry all things back to the ships. and to make themselves ready for the voyage, but because this was somewhat long a doing, the old lord commanded forth a party of his concealed soldiers, which had hitherto been planted in the wall so that we had taken no notice of any of them, whereby I observed that this tower was well guarded against opposition. These soldiers made quick work of our stuff, so that no more remained to be done but to go to supper. The table being compleatly furnished, the Virgin brings us again to our companions, where we were to carry ourselves as if we had truly been in a lamentable condition, while they were always smiling one upon another, though some of them too simpathized with us. At this supper the old lord was with us, who was a most sharp inspector over us, for none could propound anything so discreetly but that he knew how to confute or amend it, or at least to give some good document upon it. I learned most by this lord, and it were good that each would apply himself to him, and take notice of his procedure, for then things would not so often and untowardly miscarry. After we had taken our nocturnal refection, the old lord led us into his closets of rarities, dispersed among the bulworks, where we saw such wonderful productions of nature and other things which man's wit in imitation of nature had invented, that we needed a year sufficiently to survey them. Thus we spent a good part of the night by candle-light. At last. because we were more inclined to sleep then see many rarities, we were lodged in rooms in the wall. where we had not only costly good beds but extraordinarily handsome chambers. which made us the more wonder why we were forced the day before to undergo so many hardships. In this chamber I had good rest, and being for the most part without care, and weary with continual labour, the gentle rushing of the sea helped me to a sound and sweet sleep. for I continued in one dream from eleven of clock till eight in the morning.

Marginal notes:

Homunculi excitantur a cupidine.

Fuerunt illi qui decollabantur.

Conjuges induunt vestimenta ut se conspiciendos præbeant.

Conjuges vehuntur trans mare.

Musick.

Custos senex.

Turris custodita a militibus.

Custos est inspector.

Laus hujus senis.

The old man's closets.

Somnium prolixum.

The Seventh Day.

After eight of clock I awaked, and quickly made myself ready, being desirous to return again into the tower, but the dark passages in the wall were so many that I wandered a good while before I could find the way out. The same happened to the rest, till we all meet in the nethermost vault, and habits intirely yellow were given us, together with our golden fleeces. At that time the Virgin declared to us that we were Knights of the 𝔊𝔬𝔩𝔡𝔢𝔫 𝔖𝔱𝔬𝔫𝔢, of which we were before ignorant. After we had made ourselves ready, and taken our breakfast, the old man presented each of us with a medal of gold. On the one side stood these words—

Hospites deponunt vestes lugubres.
Salutantur equites.
Donantur a sene.
Ars naturæ ministra.
Temporis natura filia.

AR. NAT. MI.

On the other these,

TEM. NA. F.

exhorting us to enterprize nothing beyond and against this token of remembrance. Herewith we went forth to the sea, where our ships lay so richly equipped that it was not well possible but that such brave things must first have been brought thither. The ships were twelve in number, six of ours and six of the old lord's. But he betook himself to us in our ship, where we were all together. In the first the musitians seated themselves, of which the old lord had also a great number. They sailed before us to shorten the time. Our flags were the twelve celestial signs, and we sate in Libra. Besides other things our ship had a noble and curious clock which showed us all the minutes. The sea was so calm that it was a singular pleasure to sail, but that which surpassed all was the old man's discourse, who so well knew how to pass away our time with wonderful histories that I could have been content to sail with him all my life. The ships passed on, and before we had sailed two hours the mariner told us that he saw the whole lake almost covered with ships, by which we conjectured they were come out to meet us, which proved true, for as soon as we were gotten out of the sea into the lake of the aforementioned river, there stood in to us five hundred ships, one of which sparkled with gold and pretious stones, and in it sate the King and Queen, with lords, ladies, and virgins of high birth. As soon as they were well in ken of us the pieces were discharged on both sides, and there was such a din of trumpets, shalms, and kettle-drums, that all the ships upon the sea capered again. As soon as we came near, they brought about our ships together and so made a stand. Old Atlas stepped forth on the King's behalf, making a short but handsom oration, wherein he wellcomed us, and demanded whether the royal Presents were in readiness. The rest of my companions were in an huge amazement whence this King should arise, for they imagined no other but that they again must awaken him. We suffered them to continue in their wonderment, and carried ourselves as if it seemed strange to us too. After Atlas' oration out steps our old man, making somewhat a larger reply, wherein he wished the King and Queen all happiness and increase, after which he delivered a curious small casket, but what was in it I know not. It was committed to the custody of Cupid, who hovered between them both. After the oration they again let off a joyful volle of shot, and so we sailed on a good time together, till we arrived at another shore, near the first gate at which I first entred. At this place there attended a great multitude of the King's family, together with some hundreds of horses. As soon as we were come to shore and disembarqued, the King and Queen presented their hands to all of us, one with another, with singular kindness, and so we were to get up on horseback. Here I desire to have the reader friendly entreated not to interpret the following

Navis, 1.

Vexilla 12 sign. Navis autoris libra. Horolog.

Facundia senis.

Obviatio ex arce.

500 Naves.

Applausus.

Atlas oratione excipit hospites.

Atlanti respondet senex.

Regiis conjugibus donum affert Cupido.

narrations to any vain glory of mine, but to credit me that had there been not a special necessity in it, I could well have concealed the honour which was shewed me. We were all distributed amongst the lords, but our old lord and I, most unworthy, were to ride even with the King, each of us bearing a snow-white ensign with a Red Cross. I indeed was made use of because of my age, for we both had long grey beards and hair. I had besides fastened my tokens round about my hat, of which the young King soon took notice, and demanded if I were he who could at the gate redeem these tokens. I answered yes in the most humble manner, but he laughed on me, saying there henceforth needed no ceremony, I was HIS Father. Then he asked me wherewith I had redeemed them. I answered, "With Water and Salt," whereupon he wondred who had made me so wise, upon which I grew somewhat more confident and recounted how it had happened to me with my Bread, the Dove, and the Raven; he was pleased with it, and said expressly, that it must needs be that God had herein vouchsafed me a singular happiness. Herewith we came to the first gate, where the porter with the blew cloaths waited, bearing in his hand a supplication. As soon as he spied me even with the king, he delivered me the supplication, most humbly beseeching me to mention his ingenuity before me towards the King; so, in the first place, I demanded of his majesty what the condition of this porter was, who friendly answered me, that he was a very famous and rare astrologer, always in high regard with the Lord his Father, but having on a time committed a fault against Venus, and beheld her in her bed of rest, this punishment was imposed upon him, that he should so long wait at the gate till some one should release him from thence. I replyed, "May he then be released?" "Yes," said the King, "if anyone can be found that hath as highly transgressed as himself, he must stand in his stead, and the other shall be free. This word went to my heart; conscience convinced me that I was the offender, yet I held my peace and delivered the supplication. As soon as the King had read it, he was mightily terrified, so that the Queen, who, with our virgins and the other queen whom I mentioned at the hanging of the weights, rid behind us, asking what the letter might signifie; but he, putting up the paper, began to discourse of other matters, and in about three hours we came quite to the Castle, where we alighted and waited upon the King into his hall, who called immediately for the old Atlas to come to him in a little closet, and showed him the writing. Atlas made no long tarrying, but rid out to the porter to take better cognizance of the matter, after which the young King, with his spouse and other Lords, Ladies, and Virgins sate down. Then began our Virgin highly to commend the diligence we had used, and the pains and labour we had undergone, requesting we might be royally rewarded, and that she henceforth might be permitted to enjoy the benefit of her commission. The old lord stood up too, and attested the truth of all that the Virgin had spoken, and that it was but equity that we should on both parts be contented. Hereupon we were to step out a little; it was concluded that each man should make some possible wish, and were to consider of it till after supper. Meantime the King and Queen, for recreation's sake, began to play together. It looked not unlike chesse, only it had other laws, for it was the vertues and vices one against another, where it might be ingeniously observed with what plots the vices lay in wait for the vertues, and how to re-encounter them again. This was so properly and artificially performed that it were to be wished that we had the like game too. During the game in comes Atlas again, and makes his report in private, yet I blushed all over, for my conscience gave me no rest. The King presented me the supplica-

Honor delatus autori cum sene equitat juxta Regem.

Pater. Tesseras solvit sale et aqua.

Primus custos. Ob, visam venerem factus portitor.

Autor ejusdem delicterus traditur à portitore.

Actus in Arce.

Virg. lucif.

Ludus Regis cum Regina.

Artificios.

tion to read, the contents whereof were to this purpose: First the writer wished the King prosperity and peace, and that his seed might be spread far and wide. Afterwards he remonstrated that the time was now come wherein, according to the royal promise, he ought to be released; because Venus was already uncovered by one of his guests, for his observations could not lie to him, and that if his Majesty would please to make strict and diligent enquiry, in case this should not prove to be, he would remain before the gate all the days of his life. Then he humbly sued that, upon peril of body and life, he might be present at this night's supper, being in good hopes to spye out the offender and obtain his wished freedom. This was handsomely indited, and I could well perceive his ingenuity, but it was too sharp for me, and I could well have endured never to have seen it. Casting in my mind whether he might perchance be helped through my wish, I asked the King whether he might not be released some other way, but he replyed no, because there was special consideration in the business, but for this night we might gratify his desire, so he sent one forth to fetch him in. Mean time the tables were prepared in a spatious room, in which we had never before been, which was so compleat that it is not possible for me to describe it. Into this we were conducted with singular ceremony. Cupid was not present, for the disgrace which had happened to his mother had somewhat angered him. In brieff, my offence, and the supplication which had been delivered, were the occasion of much sadness, for the King was in perplexity how to make inquisition amongst his guests. He caused the porter himself to make his strict surveigh, and showed himself as pleasant as he was able. Howbeit, at length they began again to be merry, and to bespeak one another with all sorts of recreative, profitable discourses. The treatment and other ceremonies then performed it is not necessary to declare, since it is neither the reader's concern nor serviceable to my design, but all exceeded more in invention than that we were overcharged with drinking. This was the last and noblest meal at which I was present. After the bancket the tables were suddainly taken away, and certain curious chairs placed round in circle, in which we, together with the King and Queen, both their old men, the Ladies and Virgins, were to sit. After this a very handsom Page opened the above mentioned glorious little book, when Atlas, immediately placing himself in the midst, bespoke us to the ensuing purpose:—That his Royal Majesty had not yet committed to oblivion the service we had done him, and therefore by way of retribution had elected each of us Knights of the Golden Stone. That it was, therefore, further necessary not only once again to oblige ourselves towards his Royal Majesty, but to vow upon the following articles, and then his Royal Highness would likewise know how to behave himself towards his high people. Upon which he caused the Page to read over these articles :—

I. You, my Lords the Knights, shall swear that you will at no time ascribe your order either unto any Devil or Spirit, but only to God, your Creator, and His hand-maid Nature.

II. That you will abominate all whoredom, incontinency, and uncleanness, and not defile your order with such vices.

III. That you, through your talents, will be ready to assist all that are worthy and have need of them.

IV. That you desire not to employ this honour to worldly pride and high authority.

V. That you shall not be willing to live longer than God will have you.

Marginal notes:

Supplicatio portitoris traditum autori.

Triclinium preciosissimum.

Cupido iratus ob venerem visam ab autore. Etiam Rex condolet. Lætitia discumbentium

Post cœnam obligantur equites legibus suis.

Privilegia.

At this last article we could not choose but laugh, and it may well have been placed there for a conceit. Now, being sworn them all by the King's scepter, we were afterwards, with the usual ceremonies, installed Knights, and, amongst other privileges, set over ignorance, poverty, and sickness, to handle them at our pleasure. This was afterwards ratified in a little chappel, whither we were conducted in procession, and thanks returned to God for it. There I also at that time, to the honour of God, hung up my golden fleece and hat, and left them for an eternal memorial. And because every one was to write his name there, I writ thus :—

Summa Scientia nihil Scire,
Fr. CHRISTIANUS ROSENCREUTZ.
Eques aurei Lapidis.
Anno. 1459.

Jam postulantur depositiones optionum.

Others writ differently, each as seemed him good; after which we were again brought into the hall, where, being sate down, we were admonished quickly to bethink ourselves what every one would wish. The King and his party retired into a little closet to give audience to our wishes. Each man was called in severally, so that I cannot speak of any man's proper wish; but I thought nothing could be more praiseworthy than, in honour of my order, to demonstrate some laudable vertue, and found that none at present could be more famous and cost me more trouble than gratitude; where-

Autor optat liberationem portitoris e gratitudine.

fore, not regarding that I might well have wished somewhat more agreeable to myself, I vanquished myself, and concluded, even with my own peril, to free the porter, my benefactor. Being called in I was first demanded whether, having read the supplication, I had suspected nothing concerning the offendor, upon which I began undauntedly to relate how all the business had passed, how, through ignorance, I fell into that mistake, and so offered myself to undergo all that I had thereby demerited. The King and the

Autor reus confitens.

rest of the Lords wondred mightily at so un-hoped for confession, and wished me to step aside a little; and as soon as I was called in again, Atlas declared to me that, although it were grievous to the King's Majesty that I, whom he loved above others, was fallen into such a mischance, yet, because it was not possible for him to transgress his ancient usages, he knew not how else to absolve me but that the other must be at liberty and I placed in his stead; yet he would hope that some other would soon be apprehended, that so I might be able to go home again. However, no release was to be hoped for till the marriage feast of his future son. This

Audit sententiam.

sentence near cost me my life, and I first hated myself and my twatling tongue in that I could not hold my peace; yet at last I took courage, and, because I considered there was no remedy, I related how this porter had bestowed a token on me and commended me to the other, by whose assistance I stood upon the scale, and so was made partaker of all the honour and joy already received. And therefore now it was equal that I should

Laus beneficii portitoris.

show myself grateful to my benefactor, and was willing gently to sustain inconvenience for his sake, who had been helpful to me in coming to so high place; but if by my wish anything might be effected, I wished myself at home again, and that so he by me, as I by my wish, might be at liberty. Answer was made me, that

Laudatur à Rege.

the wishing stretched not so far, yet it was very pleasing to his Royal Majesty that I had behaved myself so generously, but he was affraid I might still be ignorant into what a miserable condition I had plunged myself through this curiosity. Hereupon the good man was pronounced free, and I, with a sad heart, was fain

Reliqui læti evadunt.

to step aside. The rest were called for after me, and came jocundly out again, which was still more to my smart, for I imagined no other but that I must finish my life under the gate. I had also many pensive thoughts running in my head as to what I should yet undertake, and wherewith to spend the time. At length I considered that I was now old, and, according to the course of Nature, had few more years to live, that this anguish and melancholy life would easily dispatch me, and then my doorkeeping would be at an end, and that by a most happy sleep I might quickly bring myself into the grave. Sometimes it vexed me that I had seen such gallant things, and must be robbed of them; sometimes it rejoyced me that before my end I had been accepted to all joy, and should not be forced so shamefully to depart. Thus this was the last and worst shock that I sustained. During these my cogitations the rest were ready, wherefore, after they had received a good night from the King and Lords, each was conducted into his lodging, but I, most wretched man, had nobody to show me the way and yet must suffer myself to be tormented. That I might be certain of my future function, I was fain to put on the Ring which the other had worn. Finally, the King exhorted me that, since this was the last time I was like to see him in this manner, I should behave myself according to my place, and not against the Order, upon which he took me in his arms and kissed me, all of which I understood as if in the morning I must sit at my gate. After they had all spoken friendly to me, and at last presented their hands, committing me to the divine protection, I was by both the old men—the Lord of the Tower and Atlas—conducted into a glorious lodging, in which stood three beds, and each of us lay in one of them, where we yet spent almost two, &c.

Here are wanting about two leaves in quarto, and he (the author hereof), whereas he imagined he must in the morning be door-keeper, returned home.

Marginal notes:
Autor melancholiat.
Spes.
Metus.
Solatium.
Autor accipit annulum.
Auter dormit cum atlante & sene custode Turris.

www.ingramcontent.com/pod-product-compliance
Lightning Source LLC
LaVergne TN
LVHW061224060426
835509LV00012B/1417